HOW TO MAKE MONEY IN YOUR KITCHEN

HOW TO MAKE MONEY IN YOUR KITCHEN

by Jeffrey Feinman

William Morrow and Company, Inc.
New York

Printed in the United States of America.

1   2   3   4   5   6   7   8   9   10

Library of Congress Cataloging in Publication Data

Feinman, Jeffrey.
    How to make money in your kitchen.

        Bibliography: p.
        Includes index.
        1. Cookery. 2. Self-employed. 3. Small business.
I. Title.
TX652.F44   658'.91'642   77-3654
ISBN 0-688-03213-3
ISBN 0-688-08213-0 pbk.

Book Design   Carl Weiss

CONTENTS

CONTENTS

INTRODUCTION

There may be gold in your kitchen.

Are you happy when you're working there? Does it seem to be one of the favorite rooms for your family and friends who come to visit?

Do you feel a certain satisfaction in frosting a cake so perfectly that it's a work of art, or in having guests ask for your own special cookie recipe, or in recycling cans and bottles into useful items?

If your answers are "yes," you might be sitting on a vein of pure gold. Your talents in the kitchen could result in an exciting and enriching career that takes just as much or just as little time as you wish to give to it.

There are dozens of money-making businesses that you can start in your own kitchen. If you've been thinking about entering the job market but don't know where to go or what to do, stop and examine your kitchen and how you function in it.

Investigate the possibilities and you'll find there are

some amazing success stories of women whose kitchen industries grew into full-fledged business operations. Depending on your ambitions and persistence, you can develop a career that allows you to add extra income to the family budget or you could become an entrepreneur and build a business empire.

In the following pages we outline areas where *you* might find gold in your kitchen. This is not a step-by-step manual on how to set up any specific kitchen business. Rather, it is a guide to the many areas you can explore before going into business for yourself. And, at the end, is a bibliography of books that will help you do serious research and that will provide practical how-to information in the area you choose for yourself.

J.F.

Part I

PROSPECTING FOR GOLD IN YOUR KITCHEN

THE KITCHEN
BUSINESSWOMAN

If you've ever considered the possibility of going back to work and then given it up because (1) you couldn't or didn't want to work full time; (2) you felt the financial returns from a part-time job weren't worth the time invested; (3) your business skills were rusty or you had none at all; (4) you weren't sure just what you'd be interested in doing; or if you gave up for any other reason and yet still feel you'd like to *do* something, then a kitchen business might just be for you.

With enthusiasm, resourcefulness, and the ability to organize your time and efforts effectively, running a business from your home is not only possible, it's profitable.

Mind-boggling as starting your own business might seem, the most essential element is confidence in yourself and the product and service you offer. Just remember that you don't have to create a million-dollar conglomerate or even a full-time job for yourself.

True, people have had enormous success stemming from their kitchen endeavors, but the delightful thing about a kitchen business is that it can need very little financial investment; it can be small, yet still be profitable.

Before deciding on the type of business you want to start and going into the technical aspects of setting it up, you should ask yourself some important questions.

The following ten questions were developed by the Small Business Administration, an agency of the federal government, which was set up specifically to help small businessmen and women:

> —Are you a self-starter?
> —How do you feel about and
>   relate to other people?
> —Can you lead others?
> —Can you take responsibility?
> —How good an organizer are you?
> —How good a worker are you?
> —Can you make decisions?
> —Do people trust you?
> —Can you stick with it?
> —How good is your health?

Positive answers to most of these questions are an indication that you are capable of running your own business. If you're a woman who functions well and happily in your role as homemaker, you'll probably rate quite high in those qualities needed to run a business.

Which takes you back to your main question. You're

qualified to run a business; now how do you put your talents to work for you in a way that is both financially rewarding and emotionally fulfilling?

Consider the basic operational methods of running your own business first. There are three types of business ownership: individual proprietorship; partnership; and incorporation.

In their initial stages, most small businesses are best run under individual proprietorship, but you should be aware of the advantages and disadvantages of each type.

INDIVIDUAL PROPRIETORSHIP

The advantages: fewer tax complications, a minimum of government regulation, and flexibility in operation. You sign all the contracts in your own name, report all the income on your personal tax return. On the other hand, you also take personal responsibility for business debts, and you sometimes pay more in taxes than you would if you were incorporated. This type of ownership is best for a very limited or part-time venture where little capital outlay is needed. There is always time to incorporate when you grow.

PARTNERSHIP

If the business you choose requires help, you may want a partner. Partners pool both their resources and their talents to run the business and share, according to the terms of the partnership agreement, in its profits. Each partner reports on her personal tax form her share of the income and is personally liable for all the debts of the business.

CORPORATE OWNERSHIP

A corporation is a statutory form of organization, a separate entity under the law. Ownership is represented by shares of stock. As an entity, the corporation sells or transfers stock to obtain new capital. It signs contracts, initiates law suits, and owns property.

One big advantage to incorporating is that personal liability is limited. In addition, if such an arrangement is to your benefit, you may elect to report your share of the corporation's taxable income on your personal tax return, thus avoiding a corporate tax.

No matter how small you plan your home business to be, your first step should be to consult a tax accountant and/or lawyer to ensure that all the legal details in establishing a business are covered.

Another important person to contact is your insurance agent. Your fire insurance may need to be increased and product liability and other types of insurance may be necessary.

Other aspects of starting a business that you will have to check into include:

ZONING

Many neighborhoods have zoning limitations on the types of businesses you can operate from your home. Find out what restrictions, if any, apply to the type of business you have in mind. If you are selling your home-cooked wares or craft items by mail or to friends and neighbors, you probably will have little or no difficulty. Not all types of at-home work are subject to zoning regulations, especially if you don't identify your home as a place of business, put up signs, or hire help. In some cases where a restriction for business applies to a neighborhood, you may be able to obtain a variance from the zoning board since you are really not an "industry." With enough desire and a little resourcefulness, you can most likely work out any zoning snags you may run into in starting your business.

LICENSES AND PERMITS

Many service and food businesses require either a license or permit from the city or state. Your lawyer should be able to advise you on this, but you can also obtain the information from the county clerk's office. Most licenses or permits are easily obtained by filling in a short application and paying a modest fee. This can usually be done in a few minutes (without a lawyer).

RECORD AND BOOKKEEPING

No matter how you set up your business, the Internal Revenue Service is your silent partner. But, while taxes are the most obvious reason for keeping records, they are not the only one. To price your product or service properly, you have to know how much ingredients, advertising, and distribution are costing you. You have to estimate the cost of your time. You may need new equipment and the cost should be amortized. Then there are supplies, packaging, insurance, interest on a bank loan, if necessary, proportionate allowances for light, gas, telephone, rent (overhead), which must all be considered in the cost of producing your product . . . and which allow you to claim certain deductions on your income tax.

You can set up a simple bookkeeping system on your own. There are lots of books in the library that will aid you in working out a system for your business and all the proper record-keeping supplies are available at a local stationery store. On the other hand, if setting up the system throws you, have your accountant set up your records. Then all you have to do is write in the numbers . . . and learn to read them.

That's right. Your records tell you lots of important things you should be aware of as your business grows.

For example your bookkeeping should give you answers to some of the following questions:

1 / How much business am I doing?

---

2 / What are my expenses? Which expenses are too high; why?

3 / What is my gross profit margin? My net profit?

4 / Am I losing money on servicing some accounts?

5 / How much and how quickly am I collecting on my charge business; are slow payers costing me money?

6 / How much working capital do I have? Is it enough?

7 / What is my cash flow over an extended period?

8 / How much do I owe my suppliers?

9 / What is my net worth; the bottom-line value of my ownership in the business?

10 / What are the trends I see from my receipts, expenses, profits, and net worth?

11 / How do my assets compare with what I owe? What is the percentage of return on my investments?

12 / How many cents out of each dollar of sales are net profit? Can I increase my profits without expanding business or charging more simply by being more efficient?

BANKING

You will want to open a separate bank account for your business transactions. It's important to keep all your business transactions separate from your personal banking. It's also important to establish a personal relationship with your banker. Not only can he or she give you valuable advice, but as your business grows you may need business loans—short or long term—and it's much easier if your business is already known to the bank.

HELP:
IT'S EVERYWHERE

The success or failure of running your own business often depends on knowing just where to go for information.

No matter what type of venture you embark upon, there is a veritable sea of information available. Information that can keep you from making mistakes; information that can steer you in more creative and profitable directions.

It's all expert advice . . . and it's yours, FREE, or for a very minimal fee.

Government agencies are probably your best source. The U. S. Department of Commerce is one valuable source. Their publishing list includes innumerable publications which analyze various businesses. These fact sheets and management pamphlets can give you valuable insights that will aid you in running your business.

You can write to Washington, D. C., but there are 42 field offices throughout the United States; some of them offer help for small businesses and two of them (New York and Massachusetts) have special women's programs sponsoring a series of seminars at which experts advise on how to price, market, and package home products and services. If a field office isn't listed in your yellow pages, call your local Chamber of Commerce for the address and telephone number of the nearest one.

Be specific in requesting information. Explain what you plan to do and outline your objectives briefly. The more details you provide, the more helpful the office can be in providing printed materials or other information. The Small Business Administration can also be invaluable. This agency was set up to help small businesses grow and prosper.

SBA offers printed materials and advice on almost every conceivable facet of business planning. Consult the classified telephone directory or your Chamber of Commerce for the address and telephone number of the SBA office nearest to you, or write directly to the Small Business Administration, Washington, D. C., for this information.

Your local SBA office can provide you with useful guidelines for setting up your business. It can also pull out the reference material you'll need on advertising, record-keeping, marketing, loans, and tax benefits. Printed materials are usually FREE, but there may be a minimal charge for some booklets.

Most important, your local SBA people can help you to analyze the need for your particular kind of business in your area and can make suggestions that might save you time and money. If you just want to do some research on your own before proceeding at all to set up a small business, request the lists of publications issued by the U. S. Department of Commerce and the Small Business Administration through:

Superintendent of Documents
Government Printing Office
Washington, D. C. 20402

Don't overlook your public library as a source of good business information. Most libraries have all the directories you'll need for business research, as well as a wealth of books that might help you in developing your own kitchen product.

Librarians are the greatest treasures in a library. They know everything that's in the library or where to find what you need. Inform them of your project and ask for help. Most librarians will be more than happy to be helpful. Check at the library for the how-to books that interest you in the Bibliography of this book.

KITCHEN MARKETING

You've chosen your business. You've gone through the initial organizational stages. Now, you're ready for business. But first, to sell your product or service, you've got to tell the public it's available.

How do you do it? Start with the obvious—advertising. No matter what product or service you've chosen to sell, you've got competition for your consumers' dollar. Advertising is the quickest way to let people know what you are selling. Good advertising is essential to convince people that *your* product or *your* service is the one they should buy.

Presumably you will have given a great deal of thought to the name you choose for your business. It may tell what it is, like "Caroline's Candy Kitchen," or it may be an intriguing name such as "The Kitchen Potpourri" which leaves a lot to the imagination. Whatever the name, your advertising copy must tell a potential buyer what you have to sell and why he or she should buy the item from you.

Remember that you start out with one of the *best* current selling points: Your products are homemade; your services are individualized and personal. Establish these points in your advertising immediately.

After a little research you can write your own advertisements. Start out by listing all the selling points you want to make. Then look through your local newspapers and cut out the advertisements that intrigue and interest you. Study them and base your own copy on those that seem best to you. Don't copy. You've got your own story to tell. Just use the good advertisements as examples to guide you.

Very often the advertising people at your local paper can help you to prepare your advertisement and can even provide you with art work. Talk to them before you go ahead. Which brings us to where you should place your advertisements. Ask for advertising rates and circulation information from local weeklies, "shoppers," and small dailies. Then base your choice on the number of people the paper reaches and the neighborhoods they live in. If a daily covers the entire city, but you really just want to reach those people within your neighborhood, the local "shopper" might be best for you. Advertising to people who don't need or will never use your services is a misuse of your advertising budget.

On the other hand, a listing in the yellow pages of your telephone directory is an excellent way to reach people, even though the directory may go into territory you ordinarily wouldn't reach as well as your own. With a business phone—and no matter how small your business, you should have one—you are entitled to a free listing in the yellow pages. A display ad costs, but it does stand out to attract the attention of those cussumers who are looking for the type of product or service you offer. An advertisement in the yellow pages also lends your business an air of permanence and stability.

Don't overlook employee magazines, club newsletters, and local theater programs as advertising vehicles. They are usually quite inexpensive and may go to just the audience you should be reaching.

Local radio spots are also effective for certain kinds of businesses.

Direct-mail advertising can also be effective. Here you can really choose the market you reach. You can mail to every house in your neighborhood; to all the executives in the manufacturing plants; to mothers of school-age children; to the members of an organization; or to any specific group you choose. You can develop the list by using the telephone book; getting personnel lists from industries in your town; asking the group to send out your materials in their monthly mailings or in some cases by "buying" the list.

Your direct-mail piece can be as simple as a reprint of your newspaper advertisement with a covering sales letter and, if applicable, an order form, or it can be a brochure developed specifically for mailing.

Posters and broadsides posted throughout the area you wish to sell in are also good ways of attracting attention. Very often bulletin boards exist just for that purpose in supermarkets, launderettes, church social halls, libraries, town halls, beauty salons, and other well-trafficked places.

Church-affiliated organizations such as women's guilds and sodalities, social groups such as the Junior League, and charitable organizations such as Community Funds or the Red Cross very often have mailings, publications, or meetings to which they welcome speakers, all of which might provide new channels through which you can market your products.

Many neighborhoods have organizations to acquaint new residents with services available in the area. If there is a Welcome Wagon hostess or similar organization hostess, supply her with brochures and information to distribute to newcomers.

Also, remember that publicity differs from advertising in that it is "free." Talk to the editor of your weekly newspaper about the new business you are starting. It may be worth a story. And, if your business grows, keep that editor informed. The fact that you're providing a service that's needed and your business is growing may be worth an additional story.

Look for opportunities to appear before groups and tell them about your business; how you started it; what you offer; how it's growing. All of this spreads the word, which brings us to "word-of-mouth" publicity. Nothing beats a good recommendation from satisfied customers. Call upon your friends, family, and neighbors to help spread the word about your business. It works.

The possibilities for advertising, promotion, and publicity are endless. For the inexperienced, there's lots of help available to help you learn the techniques quickly enough for your purpose. The Business Information section of your library should have a number of books on marketing and advertising.

THE CHOICE IS YOURS: HOW TO MAKE A GOOD ONE

The idea of a kitchen business is intriguing. You'd like to work in your own home. The idea of cooking, baking, and being inventive in your own kitchen has appeal for you. Now it's time to think about matching your skills with the best opportunity to make money.

Inspiration may hit you. The timing, circumstances, and details of setting up a catering service, a cookie bakery, or a tearoom may all seem to fall into place. Intuitively you know that your inspiration was "meant to be" and chances are you can almost count on success. In actuality, you probably had that thought or concept tucked away in the back of your head just waiting for the "go"signal. You're set. You've got an idea. Now all you have to do is make it work.

Or chances may be that you, like many women embarking on a career, aren't quite sure of just exactly what you want to do. You're a creative cook; you like to entertain; you like making things; you like people, but how can you make any of that or all of that work for you in a business?

Try the business analyst's standby. Make lists. Add up the pros and cons.

Think it all out.

What do you enjoy doing most in the kitchen? Baking pies? Do your pies look as good as they taste? Do you have enough equipment to bake large numbers of pies? If you need additional equipment, do you have space and how much will the equipment cost? Is there an excellent bakery in the neighborhood or are the choices only between the frozen and the commercial bakery products in the supermarket? Is it the kind of neighborhood where entertaining is a way of life and people would be willing to pay a fair price for the product you produce? Are there restaurants within a radius for delivery that might like to feature homemade pies for desserts?

When you sit down with pencil and paper you'll think of even more questions. Put down the answers to them all—pro or con.

When you're finished, if making pies has more going for it than against it, you may have found the vein of gold in your kitchen that will pay off for you.

Part II

THE KITCHEN
FOOD SPECIALIST

BUILD A BUSINESS
SELLING FOOD
AT FAIRS,
FLEA MARKETS
& STREET FAIRS

There's a growing trend throughout the country. The street fair has come into its own. Even in New York you can find a street fair, one or two blocks long, on almost every Saturday or Sunday. In fact, on one Sunday, on the West Side we found three street fairs within a ten-block area. These street fairs are city versions of the suburban garage sale, but with some professional touches added. As for garage sales, the big question in many suburbs is "Where are the sales this weekend?" Flea markets are fun, too. They seem to be the American version of the Middle-Eastern *souk* and while the local market may lack the mystery and excitement of an Arabian bazaar, good cooking, international fare, and old-fashioned ingenuity give it its own special flavor.

Add to these the church, school, or organization bazaars and you've found an opportunity to earn money on a more or less regular basis by selling a product in a friendly, informal atmosphere.

If you systematically go about discovering the locations and dates of these events within a 40- or 50-mile radius, you can probably be busy every week.

Food and drink are always big sellers at these fairs, especially if they are outdoor events where people browse and some entertainment is planned. Develop a specialty that can be prepared beforehand and heated or cooked at the event.

Or, you might want to sell homemade cookies, brownies, cakes, candies, or preserves prettily packaged for people to take home.

If you prefer being a seasonal businesswoman, holiday bazaars offer the opportunity to make extra money. While many churches and organizations ask only for contributions to be sold to raise money, others have gone into the practice of sharing the profits with the participants.

Here it's wise to develop a specialty and to package your product in festive wraps. Of course the holidays provide plenty of opportunity to think of novel ways to present your items, but to start you thinking we're including instructions for making two interesting items that were snapped up at fairs we attended.

Cookie Mobiles: Make your favorite sugar cookie recipe

using Christmas cookie cutters (or any "theme" you wish) such as stars, angels, trees, stockings, and so on. Before baking, make a hole near the top of each cookie by piercing the dough with a sharp instrument. When the cookies are decorated and ready to hang, insert a string or narrow ribbon through each hole. For a "mobile" you can use pliable wire coat hangers covered with foil, ribbon, or green florist's tape. Shape the mobile however you wish and string the cookies from it, using different lengths so they will hang at various levels.

Church Windows: By using the following recipe you can make attractive and good-to-eat candy which, when sliced, gives a stained-glass effect. This is very simple to make and something that children could make, too.

CHURCH WINDOWS

12-oz. pkg. chocolate bits
1 stick butter or margarine
10½-oz. pkg. miniature colored
    marshmallows

1 cup chopped nuts
7-oz. pkg. flaked coconut

Directions: Melt chocolate bits and butter in double boiler over moderate heat and let cool. Add nuts and marshmallows. Divide into four "logs" and roll in coconut. Wrap in waxed paper and refrigerate. Slice as needed. It keeps well for weeks.

To package this candy attractively, yet cheaply, cover your container with strips of different colored cellophane. Then cut out square, triangular, or star shapes in a piece of construction paper, mosaic-design wrapping paper, or silver foil, and glue it in place over the container, making sure that there is cellophane backing each cut-out.

Empty cans with plastic lids can be used for fruit-cakes, cookies, and candies. They can be covered with an attractive adhesive-backed paper, or with pieces of felt. A versatile idea for covering empty coffee cans with felt "boot" patterns, which were featured in the November 1971 issue of *Family Circle* magazine, can be obtained by sending 1.00, plus 25¢ for postage and handling, to:

Leland Crafts
P.O. Box 1009
Reseda, Calif. 91335

Ask for Pattern #133. There are three unique designs given and no doubt you will be able to expand on these with some novel ideas of your own!

Any items you may have left over from a flea-market sale or street fair can be sold by door-to-door canvassing or left in a local grocery store if the owner is agreeable to that. Even your local cleaners may be amenable to your leaving some items in an out-of-the-way spot on the counter during the holiday season. Take advantage of the goodwill and holiday spirit permeating the air. Speaking of goodwill, you might spread some around yourself by leaving some of the leftover goods at hospitals, child-care centers, and nursing homes. It not only adds to the happiness of others, but it is a business tax write-off.

THERE'S HEAVY TRAFFIC IN THE HOLIDAY KITCHEN

Every year as Christmas approaches you'll find *Holiday Inn* scheduled for the movies on TV. The inn was Bing Crosby's dream of a place that would open only for the holidays—Christmas, New Year, Easter, Fourth of July, Hallowe'en, Thanksgiving—with a smashing show themed to the holiday, and the proprietor would then rest, relax, and prepare for the next show in between times.

If you don't quite see yourself in a day-to-day or week-to-week business but there are times during the year when you enjoy making masterpieces such as fruitcake, gingerbread houses, Easter egg bonbons, or heart-shaped cakes, and you don't feel the pressures that too many of us feel, then a Holiday Kitchen might be for you. Depending on your interest or inclination you might limit your business to Christmas or Chanukah or you might take on all the holidays. You could also limit yourself to one product—fruitcakes or gingerbread houses—or you might package cakes, candies, jams, and jellies in marvelous gift packages.

Packaging for a holiday gift kitchen is where you can let your imagination run wild and your prices go high. For example: If you stuff dates with pecans or walnuts, roll them in either granulated or powdered sugar, and sell them for $3 a dozen, boxed, you make a profit. But if you take the same dozen dates, arrange them in a crystal candy dish for which you pay (wholesale) $2.50, wrap in clear plastic, tie with a red-and-white striped bow, and stick in a piece of fresh holly as it goes out the door, you have an $8.00 or a $10.00 item.

Here are just a few ideas for a Christmas Kitchen:

FRUITCAKES

Thanksgiving through Christmas is fruitcake time, but happily you can make the cakes ahead of the season, especially if you are seasoning them with brandy.

The mechanics of starting a fruitcake business are simple. First, come up with a good recipe. It can be your Aunt Sarah's handed down from generation to generation or you can choose the one you like best from the *Fannie Farmer Cookbook* or the *Better Homes*

& *Gardens* cookbooks, or it can be one you clipped from a magazine ten years ago. Just remember that your customer's vision of fruitcake is probably rich with large chunks of fruit and lots and lots of nuts.

Your market potential for fruitcakes is quite extensive. Traditionally people feel that fruitcake is an integral part of the holidays. Most people prefer that it be homemade. Luckily for the smart businessman or woman, most people can't quite seem to "get it all together" at the holidays and have to go for help on the outside. In fact our favorite fruitcake success story is of a Marina Del Rey (California) man who started out selling his homemade fruitcakes from his kitchen and built the operation into a million-dollar business with an October 15 to December 24 selling season.

Remember, too, that holidays are one time when consumers don't like products like fruitcake to have that commercial "finished" look. They prefer the straight-from-the-kitchen look for charm.

Potential consumers include your friends, your neighbors, and your husband's and relatives' coworkers. Prepare flyers for distribution that remind them that fruitcake is not only a holiday "must" to have in their own homes but that it makes a marvelous hostess gift for holiday visiting or a pleasant token of appreciation to people they want to remember during the holiday season. Be sure to list a deadline for orders and to require a deposit on all orders.

Businesses and corporations often send holiday tokens to their clients and associates or to their employees. In fact, American businessmen spend more than a billion dollars on corporate Christmas gifts. Frequently these gifts take the form of liquor, candy, and fruitcake.

In larger businesses, corporations, or manufacturing plants, the head of personnel or the purchasing agent or the public relations manager is responsible for making these purchases. A telephone call will usually establish just whom you should be calling upon.

Your selling point here is that a homemade product is a more personalized gift than a commercial product and conveys a warmer, richer holiday feeling. Naturally, your product is better, too. Here packaging is important and you'll want to have your fruitcake look special even if you use only a glossy red box with a magnificent bow.

Remember, though, that businesses usually commit themselves for holiday gifts early, some of them as early as July, so don't wait until November or December to start selling. Except in rare instances or for smaller businesses, you'd be late.

Start first with the traditional big gift buyers: insurance and advertising agencies, commercial printers, leasing agencies, manufacturers. You can get a list of all the businesses in your area from the Chamber of Commerce.

Then cover the smaller businesses. Despite their size, they often have sizable gift lists or do give gifts to their employees.

Many businesses now have a ruling that employees

cannot accept gifts from suppliers. However, gifts of food are usually an exception to this rule. And many companies are looking for something different from the usual candies, cookies, or cocktail packs.

Don't overlook those people who sell *you* services. If you know your local insurance agent, are aware that a small businessman gives out gifts, approach them. Your fruitcakes might be a welcome change from the usual items offered.

Finally, there are the retail stores. Many stores that would never think of carrying food will consider selling gift fruitcakes for the holidays. An Omaha housewife we were told about successfully sold out her entire production of cakes through two clothing boutiques and a small florist.

The key to retail sales is profits—for the retailer. You'll have to be happy with a small mark-up, since you can't really undercut your retail distributors, at least not on single-item sales, but you do get wider distribution with little effort on your part. (If a company buys in quantity, you can offer a special price.)

Sampling is the key to selling to all of these markets. Let the buyers know just how delicious your product is by letting them taste before they buy. Make up a number of cakes for sampling purposes, slice in small pieces, wrap in clear saran.

Labeling fruitcakes can be fun, too. As we mentioned before, people like that homey look. You can handwrite your labels, rather than setting type, or have them imprinted so that they look as if each label were individually done.

In addition, if for instance you are using Aunt Sarah's recipe, you could include a little folder with the story of how the whole neighborhood used to flock to her house at Christmas to taste her marvelous fruitcake, or how she used to give out her recipe but always omitted one secret ingredient so that the resulting cakes never tasted exactly like hers.

Delivery service is also a service you can offer to gift buyers. It's an additional plus that might just help you close the sale and for which you can charge. Limit the radius in which you will personally deliver and inform people you will mail or send packages by United Parcel Service outside the area specified.

Most corporate gifts will be in a single area and you could hire a student or ask a friend with a car to handle this part of the operation.

THE GINGERBREAD WORKS

Christmas is fantasy time. Gingerbread houses, castles, and elaborate frosted cookies are favorites of children and grownups alike. If you like to combine cooking with crafts and have a marvelous imagination you can enjoy yourself creating "visions of sugarplums" to sell.

The more elaborate your creations, the more you can

charge. Pricing these items is somewhat like pricing a work of art. It all depends on how the public reacts.

For starters, check back on the old November and December issues of magazines like *Good Housekeeping, Woman's Day, Ladies' Home Journal, Family Circle, McCall's,* and *American Home* or *House Beautiful.* These magazines usually have recipes, instructions, and even plans for building gingerbread and candy houses.

You should make up several samples and have them on display in your home. You may also be able to set up displays in offices and corporations that run Christmas "stores" for the convenience of their employees and in nearby retail or specialty shops.

Also think of your gingerbread houses as displays. Local retail stores may wish to buy them for Christmas decoration. For example, how about talking your local jeweler into a window in which the gingerbread house is the focal point with a path of gold chains leading to the door, a lake of sparkling pins shining beside it, and a roof studded with pendants to wear on the chains. Or your local toy store might go for a giant house surrounded by floppy stuffed animals in its yard outside. Or your town's most elegant dress shop might fill its windows with fabulous dresses floating above a fantasy gingerbread land.

You'll want to make your houses on special order with deposits required, so start advertising and promoting early for single orders, even earlier for displays.

It may be a seasonal business, but you can earn enough to enjoy the profits all through the year.

THE SUGARPLUM SHOP

You've got two things working for a Christmas business. Everybody prefers to serve or give homemade cookies, candies, or cakes and most people aren't organized enough to find the time to make these things themselves. Most shoppers are delighted to pay a premium price if you will take the harassment out of the holidays and not leave them with no choice but to buy the banal commercially made Christmas cookies and candies.

The nice thing about cookies is that many of the recipes can be frozen so you can work ahead of schedule and just pop your goodies into the oven at the last minute. There are also cookies that seem to taste better and better if you make them ahead of the holiday and store them in tin containers.

And there are cookies that make beautiful decorations and tree ornaments.

Here again, packaging can make a difference in pricing.

You probably have favorite recipes of your own and the women's magazines and cookbooks can provide you with dozens of additional ideas and recipes, but we'd like to share a few of our favorites with you.

BUTTER
NUT
BALLS

1 cup butter
½ cup sifted powdered sugar
1 tsp. vanilla
⅛ tsp. salt
2¼ cups sifted flour
¾ cup chopped nuts

Beat butter until soft. Add powdered sugar. Stir in vanilla and salt. Add flour gradually. Work in nuts thoroughly. Chill dough one hour. Form 1″ balls. Bake on ungreased cookie sheet at 400° for 10–12 min. Dough should be set but not brown. Roll cookies while warm in powdered sugar. Cool, then roll in powdered sugar again. (This dough can be colored with red or green food coloring, if desired.)

CREAM
CHEESE
FOLDOVERS

2 cups sifted flour
¼ tsp. salt
1 cup soft butter
One 8-oz. pkg. cream cheese (softened)
Confectioners' sugar
Red jam or jelly, or apricot

Sift the salt and flour together. Cream the cheese and butter until light and fluffy. Blend in the flour mixture. Chill for several hours or until firm enough to roll. Roll to ⅛" thickness on a board sprinkled with confectioners' sugar. Cut into trapezoid shapes about 2" across at the widest part. Spread with jam or jelly. Fold over once so that sides meet. Place on ungreased cookie sheets and bake at 375° for about 15 min., do not brown. If desired, sprinkle with confectioners' sugar. Store cookies in airtight container and refrigerate. Can be frozen. Makes about 4 dozen.

WALNUT
FROSTIES

2 cups flour   ½ cup butter
½ tsp. soda   1 egg
¼ tsp. salt   1 tsp. vanilla extract
1 cup brown sugar

Combine flour, soda and salt. Gradually add sugar to butter in mixing bowl, creaming until light and fluffy. Add egg and vanilla extract; beat well. Gradually add dry ingredients, mixing well after each addition. Shape into 1″ balls. Place 2″ apart on ungreased cookie sheets. Make a depression in center of each cookie; place 1 teaspoonful of topping in depression. Bake at 350° for 12 to 14 min. Yields about 4 dozen.

Topping: Combine 1 cup chopped walnuts, ½ cup firmly packed brown sugar and ¼ cup dairy sour cream.

46

SUGAR
CUT-OUTS

¾ cup soft butter	2½ cups flour
1 cup sugar	1 tsp. baking powder
2 eggs	1 tsp. salt
1 tsp. vanilla or lemon extract	

Cream butter and sugar. Add eggs and extract; beat well. Sift together flour, baking powder, and salt. Add to creamed mixture. Wrap in plastic wrap and chill overnight. Roll out to ⅛″ thickness on floured pastry cloth. Cut out with lightly floured cookie cutters. Bake at 400° for 6 to 8 minutes.

Note: Decorate before baking with bits of candied cherries, colored sugar, and tiny candies. Or, decorate after baking with tinted confectioners' sugar frosting as follows: Blend until smooth ¼ cup butter, 4 cups sifted confectioners' sugar, ¼ cup scalded cream, 1 teaspoon vanilla.

47

PEANUT
BLOSSOMS

1 cup sugar
1 cup brown sugar
1 cup butter
1 cup peanut
   butter
2 eggs
¼ cup milk

2 tsps. vanilla extract
3½ cups sifted flour
2 tsps. baking soda
1 tsp. salt
2 bags foil-wrapped
   chocolate kisses

Cream butter, beat in sugar, brown sugar, peanut butter. Mix well. Add eggs, milk, and vanilla. Beat until well blended. Sift together dry ingredients and gradually add to batter. Shape into balls and roll in granulated sugar. Bake at 375° for 10 to 12 minutes. Remove foil from chocolate kisses and place one kiss in center of each cookie while they are still warm.

SPRITZ
COOKIES
(Cookie-press
Cookies)

2½ cups unsifted flour
¼ tsp. salt
1 cup butter (softened)
1¼ cups sifted confectioners' sugar
2 egg yolks
½ tsp. almond extract
1 tsp. vanilla extract

Place softened butter in large bowl. Add sifted confectioners' sugar. Beat with mixer or wooden spoon until mixture is light and fluffy. Beat in egg yolks, almond and vanilla extracts. Sift flour and salt together, and add to mixture. Beat until blended. Fill cookie press with dough. Place fancy cookies on ungreased cookie sheets. Bake at 375° for 10–12 min.;

do not brown. Cool and decorate with confectioners' sugar icing (see Sugar Cut-outs recipe) or decorate before baking with candied cherries or colored sugar.

ALMOND
COOKIE
CUPS

Butter or margarine (softened)
Sugar
All-purpose flour
⅔ cup slivered toasted almonds, chopped
3 tbls. heavy or whipping cream

Up to four days ahead: In small bowl with mixer at high speed, beat 6 tbls. butter with ¼ cup sugar until fluffy. Reduce speed to low; beat in 1 cup flour. Press dough into bottom and up sides of twenty-four 1¾" muffin-pan cups. Bake at 350° for 10 minutes.

In 2-qt. saucepan over low heat, heat almonds, cream, ½ cup sugar, ¼ cup butter and 4 tsps. flour to boiling, stirring constantly.

Remove from heat. Spoon some almond mixture evenly into each cookie shell. Return to oven and continue baking 12 to 15 minutes longer, until lightly browned. Cool on wire racks about 5 min. or until cookies are firm. With blunt knife, loosen cookies; remove from muffin cups, and place on racks to cool completely.

AN APPETIZING BUSINESS: HORS D'OEUVRE & OTHER TASTY TIDBITS

Of all the details that go into planning a perfect party, making the hors d'oeuvre and canapés is probably the one that most hostesses would just as soon have done for them . . . if they could just be sure that the canapés wouldn't be soggy and the hors d'oeuvre tasteless and boring.

For those parties where peanuts and potato chips just won't do, the pressured hostess might be looking for someone like you. That is, if you enjoy making a tray of food look almost too good to eat—but not quite; if you pay attention to making each tiny tidbit perfect.

Home entertaining is growing in popularity and party givers tend to be repeaters and to give bigger and bigger parties. Searching out a few good customers and keeping them pleased can be like an annuity. And, these parties can be your advertising. Unless the hostess wants to pass off the appetizers as her own, chances are that the people who attend are also party givers who would be happy to know about a service such as yours.

For this business your listing in the yellow pages under *catering* is invaluable, as is advertising in your local paper. You can also send a mimeographed circular or flyer to those neighborhoods where home entertaining is part of the life-style and to corporations and businesses that give company and promotional parties.

You might also be a subcontractor. Talk to a good local bakery, delicatessen, or specialty food shop that ordinarily supplies hostesses with food. They might wish to offer an additional service.

Examine your market and be imaginative. Universities are excellent areas in which to sell this kind of service. Student and faculty organizations are constantly running teas and parties; faculty parties are common and alumni affairs are also good.

Even urban centers with a plethora of caterers are not to be ignored. One young woman I know in New York City supplemented her secretarial income by preparing hors d'oeuvre for business and private parties. She made her contacts through her office and her sideline became so profitable that she almost decided to give up her job.

The reasons for her success: (1) good professional caterers who have already established a reputation are often booked months in advance; (2) many people in the business allow themselves to get "stale," to offer nothing new and to allow the quality of their product to decline.

Which brings us to what kind of hors d'oeuvre or canapés do you offer?

Develop a few specialties. Foods that are unique to you. Develop some things that can be frozen and heated quickly so that you can always accommodate clients who have last-minute requests. Meatballs, quiches, and miniature crêpes are great for keeping on hand, and if you have clients who always like to be prepared, you can sell your preparations to them frozen with instructions for heating. Also develop a "spectacular," something that's absolutely out of the ordinary.

This is another area where pricing has to do with presentation. If you take a loaf of pumpernickel bread, slice it, and quarter the slices, then top them with a caviar-and-cheese spread and garnish with parsley you may be able to charge up to 25¢ a piece, which is quite profitable. But take the same ingredients: Cut horizontally a whole loaf of pumpernickel bread into five or six slices; spread one slice with seasoned cream cheese; the next with cream cheese and a thin layer of caviar; continue, alternating the filling of each layer; restack in loaf form, and garnish with thin slices of lemon and dabs of cream cheese and caviar. Suggest the loaf be cut on the diagonal. You might be able to up your price and your profit by as much as 15 to 20 percent. Call it a Russian Luxury Loaf and you've got yourself a winner.

Packaging your wares is easy. You may use standard baker's boxes, disposable foil trays, plastic wraps and plastic containers. Look through the yellow pages and buy directly from the manufacturer in bulk.

You might also offer your clients serving pieces that must be returned. This means investing in attractive serving trays, chafing dishes, and bowls for dips. You'll want deposits on items like these, but they are extras that can determine the final sale.

Delivery is another service rushed hostesses will base their decision on. You can charge for this service and you should. However, establish a price limit such as no deliveries on orders under $10 or $15.

This is one area where rapid expansion is possible. A lot of the work can be done by people with no culinary skill but with direction from you. So, if a big order comes in, call upon the family to help or hire a few neighborhood teenagers who can earn as much money at this as they can baby-sitting.

54

Your major investment here may be additional refrigeration just for your business. It takes time to make these appetizers and some of the more delicate foods could spoil if left out too long. In addition, you'll want freezer space for those "at-the-ready" specialties we talked about.

Refrigeration is something to think about when you're making up your list of selections. Canapés that get soggy or foods that turn color slightly are never a good choice. Base your selection on each item's longevity, appetizing looks, and delicious taste.

Set up a test kitchen before you prepare your list. Try canapés on your friends and family and look for reactions. Test frozen foods and see how long other dips and mixes will keep properly when refrigerated.

Developing specialties is easy. You probably have a few of your own already. In addition, do some research. Here again the women's magazines and the proliferation of cookbooks are invaluable. They not only give recipes but give ideas for garnishes and serving.

Among people's favorites are shrimp and crab hors d'oeuvre, hot or cold; *pâté;* caviar, red and black; quiche; miniature meatballs; and, currently, crêpes with an assortment of fillings.

Selling appetizers could develop into a catering business, too. See the section beginning on page 103.

MARVELOUS TREATS YOU CAN PRESERVE: JAMS & JELLIES

Anyone who ever tasted a homemade jam or jelly on his morning toast is forever spoiled. As excellent as many commercial products are, mass production and the preservatives needed to prolong their shelf life somehow rob them of that unique flavor that seems to contain the sunshine of summer.

It is this quality that makes the most *common* fruits also the most desired ones for preserving. And, it's this quality which ensures that there will always be a market for such homemade products.

You could go into the jam and jelly business if you have never made preserves before, but if you've always enjoyed making and giving or serving these marvelous treats to friends and family it could be a natural for you.

However, even if you are a dedicated jam-maker with your own recipes, you'd be wise to do a little research. Jellies and jams can be made with or without pectin, from a variety of fruits and combinations of fruits. Your success in this business is based upon the quality of the fruit you use as well as the cooking, jarring, and storing.

For jelly-making you need fruits with definite flavor. More delicate flavors are diluted by the large amounts of sugar called for in the recipe to ensure the right consistency.

Also remember that while your family's favorite might be fig or red-pepper jam, it's a sure thing that grape jelly, and strawberry or cherry jam are going to be bigger sellers. You'll probably want to have some unusual combinations, but to build a business you'll need everybody's favorites.

Economics will also have an influence on the jams you make. You should buy your fresh fruits at the peak of their season, when they are both plentiful and cheapest. This means that in most parts of the country you'll do your preserving in the summer and fall months, and sell your goods during the holiday season.

Recipes abound. Choose the ones that sound best, then experiment and make them your own.

Jams and jellies are easy to sell from your home. As the word spreads, you'll find people will make their way to your door. They are also excellent mail-order items, too, especially if they have a regional flavor. If you have a specialty like Georgia Peach Conserve or Cape Cod

Cranberry-Orange Jam, you can probably build a very nice mail-order business.

If you live in a resort area, you can also probably build a very nice house and mail-order trade. But, if your locale isn't quite perfect, don't give up the idea.

A good local restaurant could welcome serving home-made preserves as a specialty and might be willing to sell your product at the front desk as well as to buy it for the restaurant's own use.

Local gourmet shops might be induced to put in a line of homemade jellies and jams with their own exclusive label on them.

Bakeries are also a good bet. What better way to sell breads and rolls than by teaming them up with good jams and jellies. Try arranging for a sampling day. You provide the jams; they provide the bread and you urge consumers to taste bite-size pieces. This is a good way to introduce your product to the public and to let customers know they can buy it at the store.

Also, remember you want your packaging to be attractive, but you don't want it to have that commercial look. If you get a good buy on assorted jars, you can package the apricot jam in clear glass and the strawberry jam in faceted jars and the peach in little round pots. Labels can be handwritten, too.

A "loving-hands-at-home" look is just what sells jams and jellies.

WRITE A
BEST SELLER:
A COOKBOOK

Cookbooks are among the leading selling books in the world. It appears that men and women have a fascination for browsing through collections of recipes. Even occasional cooks are interested in collecting "new" recipes. Little wonder that magazines show that their food sections consistently score high in readership studies.

Yet, many popular recipe books are not the products of major publishers and only a small percentage have been written by recognized chefs. Most have been written by people very much like you.

Where does the cookbook author get his or her recipes? Few, if any, people can claim to be the sole originator of every recipe they use. Most of us have adapted the recipes taken from books, magazines, and newspapers to suit our individual tastes. We also collect recipes from friends and relatives who have done the same thing. Recipes evolve with regional subtleties, and it would seem that even internationally there is an interrelationship. For instance, the French *crêpe*, Hungarian *palascinta,* Swedish *plattir,* and the Jewish *blintz* are all the ancestors of the heartier American pancake. When it comes to recipes there is a "universal" language.

If your recipes are treasured by friends and requested by dinner guests, then why not become a cookbook author. One lovely New Jersey lady we know wrote a cookbook featuring the ethnic recipes she adapted in her kitchen and parlayed her book into a career doing retail promotions for one of the largest retail stores in the area. She had no previous business experience, but she was an author and she had promoted her own book. A successful businessman we know, who prefers to do the cooking in his household, has written and sold two major cookbooks which prove to be door-openers to clients for his company.

Once you decide that you would like to write a cookbook, consider the type of recipes you would like to feature. The possibilities are many. Just take a look in any bookstore. Depending on your interests or strengths in the kitchen, your book might be a collection of your favorites entitled something like "My Favorite Recipes Collected from My Friends" or it could focus on one dish like "170 Super Salads."

"One Hundred Seventy Super Salads," you gasp. "Where would they all come from?" Sit down and divide your book into chapters on fruit salads, vegetable salads, egg salads, molded or gelatin salads, frozen salads, pasta and rice salads, meat salads, and dessert salads. You can also include a chapter on salad dressings and one on garnishes. Now start filling in your favorite recipes under each. Still missing a few? You're the cook. Experiment and come up with a few others.

You could do the same things with desserts or appetizers or egg dishes or meat loafs or berry dishes or casseroles or bread. It's your cookbook, so it's your choice.

Another possibility is to gear your book toward people who are on special diets. If circumstances have resulted in your developing super sugar-free or salt-free recipes for your family, you'll find there is a large market of people out there for this kind of cookbook.

Diet recipe books are always big sellers, too. Here you might have to call upon a home economist for help, since calorie counters like to know just how many calories they are consuming with each portion.

Or, if you have a secret for preparing nutritious foods that appeal to the younger set, that will get mothers out of the peanut-butter-and-jelly syndrome, you probably have a winner.

All the recipes in your book should be "tested." You may have been cooking a dish for twenty years using the cup from your kitchen china to measure. But a cup of an ingredient in one kitchen may not be the same thing unless you are using standard measures. You'll need standard measuring cups, a scale, and a set of spoon measures to standardize all your recipes.

You don't have to do all the testing yourself. If there is a cooking school in your area you might work out a plan with the test kitchen or the teacher. Friends could be used to "test." What you want to establish is that your recipes are reliable and that your instructions are easily understood.

Examine some of your favorite recipe books. You'll find that most of the recipes list their ingredients in the order in which they are used. You'll also find that instructions are written in short sentences covering one step at a time.

Set your recipes up in this format. Categorize your recipes into chapters and write your introductions and any other material you want to include. Remember you also need a table of contents and an index.

Now you've written a cookbook. How do you market it?

You could send it off to a publisher. If this is your choice it might be best to query first; to send a letter with the introduction and a sample chapter or two and the outline of the rest of the book. A publisher will take over the production of the book as well as the distribution and marketing. You will probably be paid an advance against a scale of royalties that will be worked out based on the number of books printed and sold.

Try the companies that publish cookbooks. You can make up your own list by going to the library and com-

---

piling the names of the publishers of the books in the food section. Be aware that there are also "vanity press" publishers. These organizations will publish **your** book if *you* pay for it. They provide you with the finished product and you do the marketing. They are legitimate businessmen, but if you are doing this as a serious professional, to make money not to spend money, you'll avoid these presses.

Many publishers complain that "there are too many cookbooks." But, many recipe books are not produced or distributed by major publishers at all. Some of my favorites have been printed by organizations and women's groups or church groups to raise money. While many of these books are a compilation of the members' recipes, they don't have to be. You might want to offer your book to your favorite group or organization on a share-the-cost-of-printing, share-the-profits basis. If you do this, you can usually depend on members of the group to act as the sales force for the book; in addition to which local merchants are quite receptive to taking in the book on consignment. A "local" book has a ready-made "local" audience.

On the other hand, you may wish to make an investment and do it all yourself. You could still work with groups, offering them a percentage from sales made through their members. Or you could handle the marketing yourself.

Small specialty food shops, gift stores, your local bookstores and even local restaurants are all potential distributors. Book stores, in particular, might take in your book on a "sale or return" basis, meaning any un-sold copies would be returned to you for a refund after a certain period of time elapsed.

But marketing and distribution may not be the hardest part of the job. To sell your book yourself, you have to handle the printing yourself.

How do you take it from the typed manuscript to the finished book? You might consider working with a local artist who will "lay out" the book for you and share the profits based on a fair percentage which will have to be worked out. You should also look for a good local printer who will understand what you are trying to do and who will work with you to produce your book.

Cookbooks do not have to be set in type. Typewriter manuscript can be reproduced and one of the most charming books we have in our collection is all in hand script.

The idea is to produce an attractive book that can be sold at a reasonable retail price. And, besides a profit for you, that price must include the cost of ingredients for testing, any assistants you hire, the cost of produc-tion, printing and binding, the cost of distribution, re-tailers' mark-up, and any promotion and advertising you do.

It's not a simple task, but a great many people have found it both pleasurable and profitable.

RECIPES CAN BE PURE GOLD, IF YOU KNOW WHERE TO SELL THEM

One needn't write a whole book to earn money with recipes. The next time you pick up a women's magazine, take a good look at the food section. That photo of a sumptuous-looking *torte* may have been concocted by a talented homemaker just like yourself—and she was paid for it! So why not join the bandwagon and start earning $$$$$ for yourself the same way? Those recipes you've been collecting from magazines didn't just fall from the sky, nor were they all prepared by the food editors. Sure, they have been tested and perhaps adapted a little by a special cooking staff, but the credit and money still goes to you for the basic idea and inspiration.

Are you aware of the fact that each month *Better Homes & Gardens* magazine publishes recipes sent in by readers? The name of the sender is included under the recipe, which also features an attractive photo of the prepared recipe and suggests what category to file it under. The pages are printed with punch-out holes to enable readers to collect the recipes in a loose-leaf book. Wouldn't it give you a sense of pride to see some of your own recipes included among these? I don't know of anyone who doesn't get some sense of satisfaction out of seeing his or her name in print.

Complete instructions are given on a separate page for entering this recipe contest. Each issue features two different categories such as Cooking with herbs/Home-made salad dressings. They offer some hints, too, to help in preparing a dish. Each month the names of the Cooks-of-the-Month are published along with the runners-up and honor roll winners. The two top winners receive $50 each, the four runners-up receive $25 each, and twelve honor roll recipients win $10. This is an on-going feature of the magazine, so you can keep sending in recipes as often as you like. Don't get discouraged if you don't make it the first few times. Persistence and confidence in your recipes will ultimately pay off.

From time to time many major consumer publications will run recipe contests. The dollar prizes are quite high, and the satisfaction of seeing your recipe printed and the full-color photograph of your favorite dish in a publication that is bought by millions of people is immeasurable.

To keep abreast of all the recipe contest possibilities make it a point to look through current publications with regularity. Ask your neighbors to pass on some of their magazines to you after they have finished reading them so you won't have to go out and buy every one. Libraries also stock some popular magazines, so check your local library, too, as a possible source.

When you start looking in earnest you also will be amazed at all the opportunities offered you by manufacturers of food products to win money using their products in recipes—and sometimes from sources you might not expect. For example, each year Seagram's V.O. Canadian Whiskey, in conjunction with *Gourmet* Magazine, sponsors an International Recipe Competition. Last year, for instance, they offered *$5,000* to the winner for a dessert recipe! The five finalists were treated to four days in San Francisco as guests of Joseph E. Seagram and Sons, Inc., where the winner of the $5,000 award was announced.

Another major contest is the annual Pillsbury Bake-Off contest which offers up to $25,000 in prize money. There are several categories and 100 prize-winning recipes are selected each year. So, even if you don't win the big prize, there are chances to win a substantial amount of money in another division. Keep your eye out for announcements of such contests in magazines and check out your supermarkets for announcements and entry blanks.

IF PEOPLE SAY THEY'D LOVE TO COOK LIKE YOU, THEN TEACH THEM IN YOUR OWN COOKING SCHOOL

Many women today would love the opportunity to improve their cooking skills, especially in the relaxed and informal facilities of a home. If cooking is your hobby and you have mastered the art of making superior sauces and gravies, flipping *crêpes* adeptly, turning out perfect omelets, or have experimented successfully in cooking with wine, why not share your knowledge with other aspiring *gourmets?* You could limit yourself to teaching a particular specialty, or plan your lessons to include a complete meal from soup to the final dessert course. This would depend on your own range of experience and talent, the amount of time allotted for each lesson, and the number of weeks involved in your course.

Each session should be not less than two hours. If your classes are demonstration classes only, you could manage by just using your kitchen facilities. However, unless your kitchen is tiny, don't rule out participation classes which do result in more response. These classes will probably call for an investment in more equipment. You would also be more limited in the number of students in each class, but you could charge more because you would be giving personalized attention and instruction. Learning by doing is more rewarding and instructive than by just observing.

Here is how one homemaker arranged a well-planned and reasonable schedule. She holds two two-hour classes a week; one meets on Tuesday and the other meets on Thursday. She does the shopping for each class in one day and prepares the day before each one. Each course consists of eight lessons. Before each lesson the class receives a mimeographed copy of the recipe to be taught that day with a suggested menu to go with it. By the end of the course each student has an impressive array of recipes and meal plans. She holds four types of courses a year. The first is a beginners' course in French cooking; the second and third are advanced versions of the first, with more elaborate dishes, such as soufflés and pastries. The fourth course concentrates on food for entertaining. This is given only as a guide. You, of course, would have complete flexibility in working out your own schedule, depending on your particular skills and the cooking preferences expressed by prospective students in your area.

Your charge for each two-hour cooking session should be at least $8.00, plus the cost of ingredients, depending on your range of knowledge, your reputation in this area, and the financial status of your potential clientele. Some cooks with an established and excellent flair for cooking command as much as $30.00 per session. You will not be able to charge a fee as steep as that as a novice but it is not out of the question for the future. One suburban housewife in Massachusetts, specializing in her native Greek cuisine, now has her own local television show. So, you never know what the future may hold! Meanwhile, when you first begin, remember to cost-account your expenses so there will be a profit for you in your fee.

RESTAURANTS NOT ONLY SELL, THEY BUY MARVELOUS THINGS LIKE HOMEMADE PIES

Homemade desserts have built a reputation for more than one fine restaurant. So, if your pies and cakes draw compliments and even dieters find it difficult to refuse a second helping, restaurants offer a potential business opportunity for you.

We recall a *New York Times* feature on a Long Island woman, mother of four, who decided to merchandise her talents as an accomplished cook. Joining with a neighbor who was also a fine cook, the woman entered into a partnership to make and sell quiches to restaurants in their area. Before a year was out, the women

71

found themselves supplying 100 Manhattan restaurants with their luscious varieties of quiche and had expanded their product line to include cheesecakes, brownies, coffee cakes, bread puddings, and a half dozen kinds of pies.

They started slowly, first experimenting with recipes to perfect them and testing the products on friends at a series of Sunday brunches. When they felt their quiche was perfection, they approached a local supermarket and received their first large order—one hundred units in five varieties. A friend then suggested selling to restaurants and arranged some interviews. They sold to six restaurants at first, then their business and reputation grew to the point where they had to purchase a second-hand commercial mixer that could make dough for 24 pies at a time and an additional freezer that would hold 150 pies. Eventually, they also bought a pie press that would stamp the dough into the right shape for the pans. This then led to the partners opening their own highly successful retail store.

Another success story we've heard of is that of two homemakers in Massachusetts who decided to pool their cooking talents and start their own catering business.

Friends and acquaintances spread the word of their great food and the business grew without advertising. It didn't take long before one of the town's more successful restaurateurs heard about the marvelous desserts made by the pair. He and his chef met with the fledgling businesswomen and, convinced of the quality of their products and their ability to deliver a daily order, decided to feature homemade desserts. Now the restaurant's patrons delight in out-of-this-world cheesecake and too-good-to-be-true pecan pie, among other things, and the women have a solid base for their catering business.

You may not have your sights set on running a full-time, highly sophisticated business, but you can see from this example that there certainly is a market for homemade desserts.

Even without friends who know people in the restaurant business, you can take the initiative yourself. If your products are good enough to sell themselves, then all you need is the enthusiasm and confidence to convince the restaurant owner or the chef that you can maintain quality and delivery.

Your desserts do not have to be unusual. Nothing is better than a great fruit pie or a rich, moist chocolate cake, though some restaurants do like to offer something out of the ordinary for desserts. But, if you're a good-enough cook to go into this business, you probably have right now one or two specials that you've built your reputation on.

You can also test in your own home those desserts that will stand up for enough hours on a dessert cart and those that refrigerate best.

Here are some recipes for desserts guaranteed to win approval.

VELVET
CHEESECAKE

18 zwiebacks, rolled into fine crumbs
3 tbls. butter or margarine
1 tbls. sugar
Two 8-ounce pkgs. cream cheese
  (room temperature)
½ cup sugar
⅛ tsp. cinnamon
½ tsp. vanilla extract
1 tsp. grated lemon peel
1 tbls. fresh lemon juice
2 eggs, separated (room temperature)
1 cup commercial sour cream
1 tbls. sugar
1 tsp. vanilla extract

Heat oven to 300°. In a bowl blend crumbs, butter, and the 1 tbls. sugar. Press into bottom of a well-buttered 9″ springform pan. Bake 5 minutes. Cool.

Blend cream cheese and the ½ cup sugar, cinnamon, the ½ tsp. vanilla, lemon peel and juice. Beat in egg yolks one at a time. Beat egg whites until stiff but not dry; fold into cheese mixture. Pour this over crumbs in pan. Bake for 45 minutes. Blend sour cream, the 1 tbls. sugar, and the 1 tsp. vanilla. Remove cheesecake from oven; spread cream mixture over top; bake 10 minutes longer. Cool cheesecake thoroughly before removing rim of pan. May be served with fruit topping.

FROZEN CHOCOLATE CHEESECAKE

Crust: *1½ cups crushed chocolate wafers*
           ⅓ cup melted butter or margarine

Press onto bottom of well-buttered 9″ spring-form pan. Bake at 325° for ten minutes.

Combine: *One 8-ounce pkg. cream cheese, softened*
           ¼ cup sugar
           1 tsp. vanilla

Mix till well blended. Stir in two beaten egg yolks, one 6-ounce pkg. chocolate bits, melted. Beat 2 egg whites till soft peaks form. Gradually beat in ¼ cup sugar; fold into chocolate mixture. Fold in 1 cup heavy cream, whipped, and ¾ cup chopped pecans. Pour this over crumbs. Freeze. Serve with whipped cream. Garnish with shaved chocolate curls.

GRASSHOPPER TORTE

5 tsps. unflavored gelatin
½ cup cold water
⅔ cup white crème de cacao liqueur
⅓ cup green crème de menthe liqueur
2 cups heavy cream
1 plain tubed angel food cake

Soften gelatin in the cold water. Set over hot water until gelatin is dissolved. Stir in the crème de cacao and crème de menthe. Cool. Whip cream until fluffy but does not stand in peaks. Continue to beat, and slowly pour the gelatin mixture in a thin stream into the cream. Beat until mixture stands in peaks when beater is slowly lifted upright. With a thread held taut between your hands (or with an electric knife) cut through angel food cake to make five thin layers, as for a *torte*. Spread layers with filling and stack. Generously frost the top of cake with filling. Chill before serving.

LEMON LADYFINGER TORTE

1½ cups sifted
   confectioners'
   sugar
½ cup soft butter
2 eggs
2 tsps. grated
   lemon peel

2½ to 3 tbls.
   lemon juice
4 dozen 4"-long
   single ladyfingers
1 cup whipping
   cream, whipped

Gradually add sugar to butter, creaming at medium speed in mixer until light and fluffy. Add eggs, one at a time, beating well after each. Gradually add peel and juice. (Mixture may look curdled.) Beat at high speed till smooth, about 10 minutes.

On cake plate, place 12 single ladyfingers, curved side down, in two rows; top with a third of the lemon mixture, then a layer of ladyfingers. Continue layers, ending with ladyfingers. Chill overnight. Frost with sweetened whipped cream. Makes 12 to 16 servings.

For more delicious recipes we recommend a new book entitled *Grandma Rose's Book of Sinfully Delicious Cakes, Cookies, Pies, Cheesecakes, Cake Rolls & Pastries* (see Bibliography).

A SPECIALTY FOOD COULD BE A SUPER SELLER IN YOUR SUPERMARKET

Do you make a specialty that draws raves?

Then you might have a product your supermarket will be happy to carry.

While shelf space is so precious that major food companies are in heavy competition for it, you still have a chance to get an up-front position and to make a decent profit.

Local supermarket managers recognize the consumer appeal of homemade products which cannot be duplicated by a commercial producer. As a small merchant, you also offer the ability to fill orders for a dozen items or less daily which means they can offer fresh goods each day.

Naturally your biggest potential for sales lies in selling a product that is unique—a pumpkin-raisin pie or granola cookies or blond brownies, but if your regular brownies are delectable and your fudge cake is out of this world, stick with them.

Packaging your product and naming it will also enhance its sales. It's always best to have a name-check and trademark the name you choose. Ask a lawyer how to do this.

You'll also have to comply with Food and Drug Administration regulations for labeling. Contact the office nearest to you and they will be helpful, providing you with all the necessary information.

Don't be shy about approaching your local supermarket manager. You have to be enthusiastic to sell him on the idea of stocking and selling your product. If need be, place the first order on a *sale or return* basis. If it's a sellout, the manager gets credit from his bosses for a good idea and you get the orders. If it's not, he hasn't lost anything and you can try again.

Try to avoid agreeing to provide your product exclusively to a single supermarket or chain unless it can guarantee a minimum order that is large enough to be profitable for you.

If possible, have the supermarket manager pay you on delivery of your product—which will provide needed cash immediately. Point out that you are a small businesswoman and immediate payment will eliminate paper work that could increase the price of your product.

Most supermarket managers will be cooperative, but if you grow and are selling to a large number of stores within a chain, your billing will go through a centralized accounting department which will probably pay you on the chain's customary basis. This could take up to 30 days after receipt of your invoice.

One consideration: The well-known Pepperidge Farm product line began in a homemaker's kitchen. You may just want a part-time business, but the bigger possibility exists.

THE STAMP OF SUCCESS: DIRECT MAIL

More than $200 million in food will be sold through the mail this year. Mail-order statistics show that food is the fastest-growing category in the business. Cookies, candies, cakes, jams, and jellies are all being sold through the mail.

Additionally, the size or geographic location of the city or town in which you live has no bearing on the success you can achieve with a mail-order business.

What does make the difference is the product you offer. Gourmet products have had good acceptance. Regional products have also sold well through the mail. Consumers love the idea of ordering maple syrups, maple candies, or maple sauces from Vermont, or getting a "Peach Pantry" box of spiced peaches or preserves from Georgia, or "Date Delights" from California. If you have a special recipe that is indigenous to your locale or a family recipe that's been handed down through the years, then you might have something that you can sell through the mail.

Be aware that the mail-order business is not an easy one. The expert is the person whose last item made him or her a fortune. No one can really tell you if your item is going to result in a bonanza or a "bust."

Mail order also calls for an investment. You can start on a shoestring and many mail-order millionaires have done so, but it gets more difficult to do so every year. And you have to be prepared to lose money as well as make it. Naturally, the more capital you invest in starting your business, the greater your opportunity for eventual success.

If you want to take a small all-or-nothing gamble, we suggest that you have at least $1,000, preferably $2,000, for openers. This will cover the cost of producing your product, preparing advertisements and buying advertising space in newspapers or magazines, and buying mailing supplies for fulfillment of orders.

The federal government has no licensing requirements for interstate mail-order items, but since you are selling food you will have to know and adhere to the federal requirements for manufacturing and labeling. You will have to check out local and state requirements for running a mail-order business under your own name as sole owner or under a name you create for your operation.

Your local Chamber of Commerce can direct you to the proper sources of information but, since you are making a sizable financial investment, we suggest that you do obtain the services of a lawyer or an accountant who can take care of all the legal details while you concentrate on the marketing and production.

While there *are* experts in the mail-order business, they would be the first to admit that picking the successful mail-order item is much like picking the winner in a horse race. You can go by previous performance. You can pick the favorites, but favorites do lose and dark horses do win by a length. No one can really tell you that you don't have a winner.

On the other hand, there are some "do's" and "don'ts" which can help you in starting and running a mail-order business.

1. DON'T start a direct-mail mail-order business unless you can afford to carry the business initially. The mail-order business is highly unpredictable and your

first attempt could be wildly successful or it could be disappointing.

2. DO decide on the food or line of foods you want to market—and stick with it. If you believe in your product, don't make the mistake of giving up too soon. If your initial effort results in a less than satisfactory response, don't immediately blame it on the product. Examine your advertisement. Does it really sell your product? Run your own tests. Present your advertisement and a revision to friends and associates and seek their reactions. Test one advertisement in a local paper and another in a second paper to get an indication of response.

Reevaluate the publications in which your advertisement ran. Are you reaching the right audience for your product? Is your advertisement being seen in the section of the country where you have the most potential buyers?

Certain publications have a reputation for mail order, while others do not have the pull. Check the publications you might wish to advertise in in *Standard Rate and Data* in your local business library. Write to each of the publications you would consider for rate information; for marketing information about their readers; for research on response to mail-order advertising.

It's important to consider timing. An ad that runs in November and "flops" might have been a runaway success in the September issue. Do some research. Talk to other people in mail order in your locale. Ask the publications for breakdowns on response.

Analyze your marketing approach. Georgia Peach Jam may not do quite as well as Aunt Pittypat's Georgia Peach Jam. Remember you're selling a food product. You've got to describe it in a way that makes the reader's mouth water; that makes him or her want to send you a check or money order for your product. And, you've got to make it easy to send that check or money order with a well-designed ad.

On the other hand, if you've really done your research and made all the moves you think best and the response is still poor, then look closely at your product. Can you make it more attractive? Have you made a wrong choice? Is it advisable to scrap it and offer another?

3. DO plan the growth of your business in a solid and deliberate fashion. You not only have to get orders, you have to fill orders. It might be best to first test your product regionally . . . not necessarily in your own region. Just remember you don't have to take on the nation in the beginning.

4. DO investigate buying a list and selling through direct mail as well as advertising your product in publications. Your list is everything. You can choose just the people you want to reach—those who buy mail order; who earn a specific income; who live in a well-defined area of the country or section of town.

The size and reliability of its mailing list is the lifeblood of a successful, continuing mail-order business. Develop your own list as soon as possible. This is where you get your repeat business and repeat business is the foundation for success.

5. DO analyze your methods that work. You may not understand why an advertisement offering your product for $3.98 pulled better than an ad offering the same item for $3.95, but stick with the price that pulls best.

6. DO remember that good service is essential. Fill orders promptly. Answer complaints or inquiries immediately. Thank your customer for making you aware of any unsatisfactory service, enabling you to avoid making similar mistakes in the future.

THE BOX LUNCH:
YOU MAKE IT,
THEY TAKE IT

When Henri Bendel, one of New York's most exclusive stores, advertises that it's selling box lunches on its ground-floor level, you can bet that "brown bagging" it is the "in" thing to do.

Box lunches can be so much more interesting than the usual sandwich or hamburger and people are willing to pay premium prices for them, as The Brasserie, an expensive New York City restaurant, discovered when it first started offering its picnic lunch several years ago. For about $10.00, midtown executives who want to eat at the desk, or to sit on the plazas of the tall buildings to sun, can lunch well.

You can be as elegant and expensive or as simple and economical as your potential consumers warrant. It all depends on what you offer, to whom, and where your business is located.

If you live near some of the new industrial parks, you can gear your product to the tastes of busy executives and office workers. Prepare flyers to be distributed at the companies listing the entire week's box-lunch menu. You could offer one sandwich and one nonsandwich selection each day. Or you could list a number of selections with corresponding prices and pack each box to order. Try to get people to order in advance. List a cutoff time for same-day orders.

If you have a station wagon, you might consider packing lunches and selling from your vehicle at factory and industrial sites, park and recreation areas, near school grounds, or at beach areas.

Check in with your local authorities before doing this. You might need a peddler's license or there may be other local regulations and restrictions.

If you live in the city, this is still a very feasible business. Ask personnel directors at major companies in a radius where you can handle delivery to distribute your flyers to employees; also offer a special conference luncheon or give special prices for company outings or parties.

Do your own market feasibility study for this kind of business. Examine the possibilities. Do you live in a resort area where you can have a good seasonal business? Is there a new industry nearby on a site where there are not many restaurants?

Can you handle delivery or will you need help? Are you willing to make a few lunches each day until you can build your business to be profitable on a daily basis?

It's one of the simplest businesses to start, calling for little more initial investment than your time and the printing of flyers.

SERVE A HOME-COOKED MEAL IN A HOMEY ATMOSPHERE— AND YOU'RE A RESTAURATEUR!

There's a phenomenon in San Francisco—in-home restaurants. Diners love the intimate atmosphere, the individually prepared specialties.

So, why should something that's so good be limited to any one area? If you love to cook, like to entertain people, and if you have the space and facilities, you might find running an in-home restaurant both fun and financially rewarding.

Needless to say, a lot of thinking, planning, and organizing is required before you serve your first commercial meal.

First step is to research how to run a restaurant; what state and local requirements you'll have to comply with; what is your potential for business.

The Small Business Association has issued a booklet, *Restaurants and Catering,* Bibliography No. 17, which can be very helpful.

Some of the questions SBA suggests the potential restaurateur ask herself or himself before planning such a business include:

—Are you located in an area that is reasonably accessible to prospective clientele?

—How many people could you seat comfortably?

—Do you have sufficient parking space for customers?

—Does the room you intend to use have an entrance apart from the regular family traffic? If not, you may have to consider taking out a loan for remodeling, since a separate entrance is required by law.

—Do you wish to hang a sign outside your home? If so, be sure to check this out with your local zoning board to see if it would be allowed.

—Do you plan to have help? This is strongly recommended (a family operation is ideal), but if it is to be a one-woman show, better keep your menus simple. Perhaps you could limit your menu to one good "meal of the day."

Depending on the size of your restaurant, you may

be able to get by with the kitchen utensils already on hand. However, you will need to invest in additional tablecloths, napkins, perhaps candles, and additional dinnerware, glassware, and silver. You should consider buying coordinated appointments to provide a distinctive and attractive look to your restaurant. Think about the kind of atmosphere you would like to create. Do you prefer a colonial setting, a French café look, a fishing village motif, or maybe a very informal, relaxed, and homey atmosphere? Whatever your preference may be and your pocketbook will allow, do give it a good deal of thought and planning—and stick to one theme. It needn't be elaborate, and if you have sewing skills you could make your own draperies, placemats, and so on.

A good example of a real family success story is the highly successful Groff's Farm restaurant in Mount Joy, Pennsylvania. The entire family—husband, wife, and their two sons—take part in running a working dairy farm and serving country-style meals of their region right in their own large dining room. It all began when Betty Groff, as a young wife, began to get restless and considered getting a part-time job in a bank. But her family didn't care for the idea of her working outside the home, especially with a young son to look after. About that time, her mother casually mentioned that a local restaurant had advertised for a Mennonite girl to cook dinners in her own home for special bus groups, perhaps 35 to 40 people at a time. Betty felt equal to the task. She had always enjoyed cooking as a young girl and had served large meals to her supercritical relatives, of which there are many! If she could pass the relatives test, Betty figured, she could please anyone. Her reputation as an excellent cook grew so that now the whole family is involved and Groff's Farm has won high praise from such notable food connoisseurs as James Beard and Craig Claiborne.

You may not have the built-in advantage of living on a picturesque, spacious dairy farm in a tourist area such as the Pennsylvania-Dutch country, but you can make the most of whatever facilities and talents you possess by careful planning and a lot of enthusiasm. The atmosphere of your restaurant will be determined by your own home and your own taste in food and hospitality.

Some restaurants thrive on simple menus, reasonably priced, that are especially geared toward families with young children. Others serve small, elegant, formal meals.

An in-home restaurant may sound charming to you, but remember that this kind of kitchen business calls for a fairly large investment in both money and time. You may decide to serve dinner only, but you'll still find yourself with a full-time job.

If you're interested but tentative about the commitment, don't hesitate to talk to local restaurant owners for information and advice. Most business people are more than willing to share experiences and give helpful pointers, especially if you aren't going into direct competition with them.

A BUSINESS NATURAL: NATURAL FOODS

It's the back-to-nature movement that has caused a proliferation of natural-foods and health stores. Bean sprouts, yogurt, organically grown vegetables are all in vogue. If you find joy in growing your own chemical-free vegetables, baking breads from natural grains, or making preservative-free foods, you have a choice of commercial endeavors.

If you have a large enough garden, you can sell your produce for premium prices. And, if you are really knowledgeable, offer classes in organic gardening to gardeners in your area. Use your garden as part of your classroom and illustrate how you can utilize everything from leaves and grass to potato peelings, coffee grounds, and eggshells for compost.

Natural-grain baked goods or health foods or juices made from organically grown fruits and vegetables are so popular today that if you excel at making them you can turn your kitchen into a natural-food retail outlet. Or, you can become a supplier to health-food stores and restaurants.

So much has been credited to natural foods, a sense of harmony, well-being and sanity, that you could also give "Cooking the Natural Way" lessons.

To give you an idea of what we mean, here are several natural-food recipes for you to add to your own collection.

PICKLED
BEETS

2 large fresh beets
  (about 1 lb.)
1 small onion,
  thinly sliced
¼ cup cider vinegar
¼ cup water or
  beet liquid

1 tbls. honey or
  raw sugar
½ tsp. salt
4 cloves
½ bay leaf

Scrub beets and trim root and stem ends without cutting into the beet. Place in saucepan with water to cover. Bring to boil, cover and cook 30 to 40 minutes, until tender. Peel and slice. Cut each slice in half. Place in shallow casserole or bowl. Combine remaining ingredients in a saucepan, bring to boil, cover, and cook 5 min. Pour cooked onions and liquid over beets. Chill 1 hr. before serving. To store, keep chilled mixture in covered jar in refrigerator. Yield: 4 servings.

THICK
BANANA
SHAKE

1 banana, peeled and sliced
1 cup milk
1 tsp. honey
¼ tsp. nutmeg
½ cup cracked ice cubes

Put the milk, honey, banana, and ice cubes into blender. Cover. Blend at high speed for about 30 seconds. Pour the shake into glasses and sprinkle with nutmeg. Serve at once.

SPINACH
SALAD

1 lb. raw spinach
¼ lb. raw
  mushrooms
4 scallions
16 cherry tomatoes

¼ lb. feta cheese
4 hard-cooked eggs
French dressing
  (recipe follows)

Wash spinach, discard tough stems, and tear remaining stems and leaves into bite-size pieces. Slice scallions thinly; wash mushrooms and slice lengthwise into thin pieces; halve each tomato. Add to spinach and toss. Crumble cheese over salad. Top with sliced egg. Pour dressing over all.

FRENCH
DRESSING

Measure ⅔ cup oil (pure unsaturated vegetable oil such as safflower, corn, soy, sesame seed, or peanut oil) and ⅓ cup vinegar into jar with cover. Add ½ tsp. dry mustard, ¼ tsp. paprika, and ½ tsp. salt. Cover and shake. Store in refrigerator. Shake well before pouring.

WHOLE-WHEAT BREAD STICKS

2 cups wheat germ
2 cups whole-wheat flour
1¼ cups milk

½ cup oil
1 tbls. honey
1 tsp. salt
Sesame seeds

Mix together ingredients in large bowl (except sesame seeds). Then, knead on oilcloth or well-floured surface until dough is easy to handle. Take a small amount of dough and roll in the palm of your hand, like a rope or coil, to form sticks ¼" thick and 5" long. Roll in sesame seeds and place on well-greased baking sheet. Bake in 350° oven for 40 minutes. Remove from baking sheet, cool and store.

BLUEBERRY MUFFINS

2 cups sifted
   unbleached flour
3 tsp. baking
   powder
3 tbls. honey
½ tsp. salt
¾ tsp. cinnamon

¾ cup milk
1 well-beaten egg
½ cup vegetable or
   nut oil
1 cup blueberries
   (cleaned and
   rinsed)

Preheat oven to 400°. Combine the dry ingredients and sift into large mixing bowl. In medium mixing bowl, mix together the beaten egg, milk, and honey. Add this mixture to the flour mixture and stir well. Add oil to batter and mix vigorously. Fold the blueberries into batter. Spoon batter into greased muffin tins, ¾ full. Bake for 25 min., or till light brown on top. Cool on rack and serve warm with honey.

A GOLDEN BUSINESS OPPORTUNITY: PLANNING CHILDREN'S PARTIES

Do other mothers enthuse about the ease with which you give parties for your children? Do they envy the way you keep all the children busy and happy? Then why not bring joy to children and relief to mothers! Go into the business of catering children's parties.

Offer to plan, buy and "produce" the entire package—the food, party theme, and decorations—including coordinating games, activities. You can also offer to provide entertainment, at a price, or to plan a special outing to a zoo or a play or ice-skating. You can also offer to provide any one or more other services. In effect, make up a party menu of services with a price list that gives mothers a break on buying the entire package.

How do you establish price? Some caterers charge by the hour, but experienced party caterers suggest that you charge by the child, plus the specific services requested as well as the time involved.

If you are requested to buy all the supplies and refreshments, keep receipts for all these expenses to be paid for by the client. Your time in shopping and expenses such as gas used in traveling to purchase these items are also billable.

Discuss the entire program beforehand to avoid unnecessary misunderstandings later on. In fact, you should outline what services you'll provide and what the charges will be in a letter to your client before beginning the party plan.

To spread the word about your service, print a flyer which explains what you offer and lists the basic charges. It's probably best to establish an age range and to indicate on the flyer that you give parties for children from three years of age to ten or eleven years. Children younger than three years have little concept of what a party is all about and are difficult to handle. Parties for three- and four-year-olds are manageable but should be kept short as their attention span may be limited. And, beyond the age of ten or eleven, children usually want nothing to do with adult-supervised parties!

As for circulating your flyer, a couple of sources to keep in mind are child-care centers and kindergartens.

Check them out to see if they have bulletin boards. They usually do. Some teachers may even agree to send a copy of your flyer home with each child since this is a child-related service. See what their policy is on this.

Now comes the fun part where your creativity and originality shine. A good children's-party caterer should have a wealth of ideas and options to offer prospective clients. Here are a few suggestions just to give you a little headway in getting started.

If the birthday child has a favorite nursery rhyme or children's storybook character, you could suggest using that character as a theme for the party. For example, if it happened to be Winnie-the-Pooh, you could co-ordinate everything from the cake, paper plates, cups, napkins, and tablecloth to hanging red balloons. If a cowboys-and-Indians theme is desired, you could make a tepee cake by using the Wilton dome-shaped doll cake pan, buy inexpensive plastic cowboys and Indians to surround the cake, and then give them to the children as favors to take home. Inexpensive sheriff's badges and plastic guns can be bought in many toy stores that feature party supplies. You could also put your own children to work by having them make paper Indian headbands to be worn by the party-goers.

Do your own children have any special interests or hobbies, such as magic? I know one mother whose 12-year-old daughter had a magic kit so she brought her along to a party with her magic act as part of the entertainment. This serves two purposes: enjoyment for the children and good experience for her daughter in learning to perform in front of an audience. The same thing could be done with puppets. Have your son or daughter and their friends work out a puppet act. For this kind of entertainment, you could charge an extra 50¢ per child which would go to the children performing the service. Also, be sure to make use of any equipment you may have on hand that would come in handy for a children's party. One mother's children were fortunate enough to win a Talking Viewmaster at a company-sponsored picnic. So for her son's next birthday she invested in a few more reels, set the family room up with chairs like a theater, and handed out plastic bags of popcorn to add to the movie-like setting.

Parties can also take the form of an outing. One mother we know of brought half a dozen children to a state park near the ocean. The park has picnic benches and tables where the birthday celebration took place. To add to the fun, they had access to swings, slides, seesaws, and so on, and were able to collect seashells in bags provided by the mother. Since the park had a jetty, the children were able to walk out on the rocks (with careful supervision). It was a wonderful party and different from the usual at-home indoor party.

Even winter parties don't have to be confined to indoors. Another mother planned an ice-skating party for her daughter and friends. She made up her own invitations in the shape of ice skates. When the skaters came back to the house, they had hot chocolate and

the birthday cake (in the shape of an ice skate, naturally) and, you guessed it—rosy cheeks.

As a children's-party caterer you could plan just such
outings, depending on where you live and what facilities
are reasonably close to you. Allow your imagination and
creativity really to work for you and you will be very
much in demand by eager mothers all around you.

THE CATERED AFFAIR:
YOU CAN MAKE
A CAREER WITH IT

If you enjoy nothing better than planning a party and
preparing for it, then there are lots of people who need
your services. Some people just can't handle all the
details.

A single successful party can start you on your career. Offices are a good place to start selling your services, especially during the holiday season. Most offices have adequate space to hold a party but little in the way of kitchen facilities. Write a letter outlining your services; include a menu, and point out that while hotel and restaurant prices are skyrocketing you can provide a more elegant repast economically in a relaxed informal atmosphere.

Catering for bridal showers, small wedding receptions, and home cocktail and dinner parties offer other possibilities. Surprising as it might seem to you, many people are traumatized by the idea of giving even a small party and are willing to pay the price for someone to help.

Most caterers prefer to do the food preparation and cooking in their own kitchens. However, it is a good idea to visit the home of the client or the locale where the party is to be held. You should know what to expect by way of working conditions and know what equipment is available to you. In many cases you will have to bring along your own tools and serving pieces.

This is one kitchen business in which it is wise to have a partner; someone who can help and fill-in in an emergency. Even the healthiest of us can come down occasionally with a virus or a twenty-four-hour flu that takes us off our feet. But all the reasonable excuses in the world will not appease a client who is relying on you to cater an important function. Choosing the right partner is a very important step and should not be done impetuously. Make sure it is someone with whom you are compatible. Two good cooks with personalities that clash will not make for a smooth operation.

Here is an example of how two homemakers started a successful catering business of their own in a city in Massachusetts. These two women had belonged to a self-initiated gourmet cooking club, comprised of a few couples who shared a fondness for gourmet food and an interest in experimenting with some different and exotic recipes. After getting to know each other well in a relaxed and social atmosphere, these two home-makers found they shared a lot in common with their interest in and knowledge of cooking. Their interests and personalities clicked, so this was the basis of their deciding to pool their talents and go into business. The community they live in is ideal for this business as the people are well able to afford frequent entertaining. This is an important factor. Also, there are a number of businesses, colleges, clubs, and so on in the immediate vicinity, so all that was needed was a few words to friends and associates and they were on their way. They have not had to spend a cent for advertising.

Beforehand they spent some time establishing some ground rules for both to follow in running their catering service; going over recipes and making duplicate copies of all recipes they intended to use, making an agreement to keep everything above board—that is, if any differences crop up, they discuss it *immediately* and

105

come to an agreement that is mutually acceptable. This makes good sense in conducting a smooth working relationship. They each keep their own books and an up-to-date listing of prices. Both keep their eyes out for special sales on ingredients used frequently, such as flour and sugar, and stock up on those items that are not perishable. No special equipment had to be purchased in addition to what they already owned.

One service they provide at no extra cost or obligation is to visit potential customers beforehand to discuss menu planning and to offer suggestions if requested. This includes help with table color schemes and decorations. Their services do not include clean-up, but they do have the names of teenagers in the area who are available for this. They insist, though, that the clean-up crew be paid independently by the client. This enables them to keep their own bookkeeping to a minimum. This system has worked out quite well for them.

Prices for catering vary throughout the country. You can charge for each dish, but you might find it more profitable and less complicated to charge a flat rate for each person.

For cocktail parties, establishing the rate you charge per person would depend on the type of hors d'oeuvre you provide. Some hostesses may have very definite ideas on what they wish to serve, while others may rely on you entirely for suggestions. You should be prepared to offer advice, should it be solicited, as to the number of canapés needed per person as well as offer assistance in working out a suitable selection. It would be good to provide variety, for instance, some hot and some cold canapés, some simple and some of the more expensive varieties (caviar, shrimp, and so forth). Determining the number of canapés to serve per person will depend on the type of function you are catering. If the guests will be having dinner following a cocktail hour, you could plan on three to four canapés per person. However, if there is to be no meal served, you should figure on more pieces and more variety, adding such things as cheese balls, dips, meatballs, and so on.

We suggest that you collate all your recipes under different categories, such as Hot Hors d'Oeuvre, Cold Canapés, Sandwiches, Chafing Dish Recipes, Sweet Finger Foods, and so on, and list them according to price. Price depends on the cost of ingredients and the time involved in preparation. The more organized you are, the more efficiently you will be able to operate your kitchen business and convince potential clients that you are the best one for the job. And remember, keep your eye out for new and interesting recipes. No matter how delicious your present repertoire may be, there are always new ideas and better ways of doing things. And if you establish a regular clientele, you will want to be able to provide them with variety and spice along with reliability.

There is not room in a book like this one to offer recipes for catered lunches and dinners, but here is a little collection for teas and cocktail parties.

LOBSTER CANAPÉS

2½ dozen 2″ bread
   rounds, cut from
   thinly sliced bread
Salad oil
One 5-ounce can
   (about 1 cup)
   lobster, shredded
½ cup canned
   condensed cream
   of mushroom
   soup

2 tbls. cooking
   sherry
1 tbls. chopped
   pimiento
¼ tsp. salt
Few drops bottled
   hot pepper sauce
¼ cup buttered fine
   dry bread crumbs

Brush bread rounds lightly with oil; put on cookie sheet. Heat in extremely slow oven (225°) 1¼ to 1½ hours or till dry and crisp. Combine remaining ingredients except bread crumbs. Spread mixture on the toasted bread rounds. Sprinkle with bread crumbs. Broil 2 to 3 minutes or till crumbs are browned. Serve hot. Makes 30.

SWEDISH
MEAT
BALLS

¾ *pound ground*
beef round
½ *pound ground*
veal
¼ *pound ground*
pork
1½ *cups soft*
bread crumbs
(3 slices)
¼ *cup milk*
½ *cup chopped*
onion

1¾ *cups half and*
half
¼ *cup finely*
chopped parsley
1 *tsp. salt*
1 *tsp. monosodium*
glutamate
¼ *tsp. ginger*
½ *to 1 tsp.*
instant coffee
½ *tsp. concentrated*
meat extract

Have meats ground together twice. Soak bread in milk five minutes. Cook onion in 2 tbls. butter till tender but not brown. Combine ground meats, crumbs, onion, 1 cup of the half and half, parsley, and seasonings. Beat vigorously till fluffy (about 5 minutes at medium speed in electric mixer). Mixture will be soft. Form into 1″ balls (for easier shaping, wet hands when necessary).

Brown lightly in 2 tbls. butter, shaking skillet to keep balls round. (Don't brown too many at a time.) Remove meat balls. Stir 1 tbls. flour into drippings; add remaining half and half, coffee, meat extract, and dash monosodium glutamate; heat and stir till gravy thickens.

Return meat balls to gravy; simmer uncovered about 10 minutes. Add more half and half if needed. Makes 5 dozen.

HEARTY
CLAM
DELIGHT

Two 3-ounce pkgs.
    cream cheese
2 tsps. lemon juice
2 tsps. grated onion
1 tsp. Worcester-
    shire sauce
3 or 4 drops bottled
    hot pepper sauce

¼ tsp. salt
One 7- or 7½-ounce
    can (about 1 cup)
    minced clams,
    chilled and drained
1 tbls. minced parsley

Stir cream cheese to soften. Add lemon juice, onion, Worcestershire, hot pepper sauce, and salt. Beat with rotary or electric beater till light and fluffy, or use electric blender. Stir in clams and parsley. Serve with crackers or chips and crisp relishes. Makes 1½ cups.

For tea-party sweet finger foods, try:

CREAM
CHEESE
BARS

⅓ cup butter   *1 cup flour*
⅓ cup brown sugar   *½ cup chopped nuts*

Cream butter and brown sugar, and add flour and nuts. Mix. This makes a crumb mixture. Reserve 1 cup for topping. Press remaining mixture into 8″ square pan. Bake at 350° for 12 to 15 minutes.

¼ *cup sugar*
8-ounce pkg.
   cream cheese
1 egg

2 tbls. milk
1 tbls. lemon juice
½ *tsp. vanilla*

Blend sugar and cream cheese. Add egg, milk, lemon juice, and vanilla. Beat well. Pour onto nut-crumb mixture, and sprinkle reserved crumb topping on top. Bake at 350° for 25 minutes. Cool; cut into bars.

CHEESE
TARTS

Graham cracker crust: Mix about ¾ cup crushed crumbs with a little less sugar and butter than you would use for a pie crust. Sprinkle these crumbs in 18 small or 12 large muffin cups (no need to pack crumbs down).

Note: Vanilla wafers may be used in place of the graham-cracker crust. Place a wafer in the bottom of small foil baking cups.

Filling:

1 egg
¼ cup sugar
¼ tsp. vanilla
One 8-ounce pkg. cream cheese

Combine and beat ingredients until smooth. Pour into muffin cups, being sure to cover crumbs or wafer completely. Bake at 375° for 10 minutes. Let cool.

Topping:

Spoon cherry, blueberry, or strawberry pie filling on top of tarts—about 1 tbls. per tart. Refrigerate. They keep for several days. May be frozen.

TEATIME
TASSIES

Pastry: Let one 3-ounce pkg. cream cheese and ½ cup butter soften at room temperature;

blend. Stir in 1 cup sifted all-purpose flour and ¼ tsp. salt. Chill for about 1 hour. Shape into 2 dozen 1″ balls; place in tiny ungreased 1¾″ muffin cups. Press dough evenly against bottom and sides.

Filling:

1 egg
¾ cup brown sugar
1 tbls. soft butter or margarine
1 tsp. vanilla
Dash salt
⅔ cup coarsely broken pecans

Beat together egg, sugar, butter, vanilla, and salt just until smooth. Divide half the pecans among pastry-lined cups; add egg mixture and top with remaining pecans. Bake in slow oven (325°) for 25 minutes or till filling is set. Cool; remove from pans. May be served with a dollop of whipped cream.

PETITS
FOURS

¼ cup butter or
   margarine
¼ cup shortening
1 cup sugar
½ tsp. vanilla
¼ tsp. almond
   extract
2 cups sifted cake
   flour

3 tsps. baking powder
¼ tsp. salt
¾ cup milk
¾ cup (6) egg whites
¼ cup sugar
1 recipe Petits Fours
   glaze

Cream butter and shortening thoroughly. Gradually add 1 cup sugar and cream together until light and fluffy. Add extracts. Sift together flour, baking powder, and salt; add to creamed mixture alternately with milk, beating after each addition. Beat egg whites until foamy; gradually add remaining ¼ cup sugar and beat until mixture forms soft peaks. Fold into batter. Bake in paper-lined 13″ pan at 350° about 30 minutes.

Cool cake 5 minutes before removing from pan. Cut cooled cake into 1½″ squares or diamonds. Line up on rack with cookie sheet underneath. Spoon or pour glaze evenly over cakes. (Keep glaze over hot water). Makes about 40 little cakes.

Glaze: Cook 3 cups sugar, ¼ tsp. cream of tartar, 1½ cups hot water to thin syrup (226° on candy thermometer). Cool to lukewarm (110°). Add 1 tsp. vanilla; gradually add sifted confectioners' sugar (about 2¼ cups) till icing is of consistency to pour. Tint with few drops food coloring, if desired. Spoon or pour icing evenly over cakes.

For pretty glaze, give cake two coats icing. (If icing gets too thick, add few drops hot water.) Pipe frosting rose on each cake or trim with candy decoration.

APRICOT
TEA
BARS

One 12-ounce jar
(1 cup) apricot
preserves
½ cup chopped
walnuts
½ cup flaked
coconut
1½ cups sifted flour
1 tsp. baking
powder
¼ tsp. baking soda
¼ tsp. salt
½ cup butter *or*
margarine
1 cup packed brown
sugar
1 egg
2 tbls. apricot nectar
1 cup quick-cooking
rolled oats

Combine apricot preserves, walnuts, and coconut; set aside. Sift flour with baking powder, soda, and salt. Cream butter in mixing bowl. Gradually add brown sugar; continue creaming until light and fluffy. Add egg and apricot nectar; beat well. Stir in rolled oats and dry ingredients. Spread half of batter in well-greased 13″ pan. Cover with apricot-nut mixture. Drop remaining batter by tea-

117

spoonsful over filling; spread carefully. Bake at 350° for 30 to 35 minutes, until golden brown. Frost warm. Cool; cut into bars. Makes 36 bars.

Note: For a moist, chewy bar, bake in a 9″ square pan. Use ¾ cup apricot preserves. Bake 40 to 50 min.

APRICOT FROSTING

Combine 2 tbls. butter, 1½ cups sifted confectioners' sugar, and 1 tsp. grated orange or lemon rind. Add 2 to 3 tbls. apricot nectar until mixture is of spreading consistency.

THE DECORATING
MAKES THE CAKE

Do people hesitate to cut into the beautifully decorated cakes you make for special occasions?

Do you frost your cakes with more flair and imagination than most retail bakeries?

Do you love to make your special-occasion cakes into works of art?

Then you have a talent to sell.

When it comes to decorating cakes, most bakeries offer standardized versions with pink and yellow roses. If you can offer something more spectacular, then you can build a very special clientele for your products.

Start off by talking to caterers. Show them good photographs of the more elegant and unusual of your creations. Offer to create cakes for them to custom order.

119

Don't be afraid to go to bakeries to offer your special decorating services. Remember that the more beautiful and unique the cakes they can offer to their customers, the more specialized business they can count on.

Advertise your services in local papers, on bulletin boards in supermarkets, and at community centers. Go to retailers who sell party goods and ask them to put up signs, provided by you, advertising your services. You can offer a commission for any orders that are taken by them.

Remember that the more special and unusual your creations, the higher the price you can command. You may want to perfect your decorating techniques by attending advanced classes.

As you become more proficient and your reputation grows, you may also give decorating classes in your home. It's an art that many homemakers would like to master at least on an elementary scale. You needn't teach them to be as adept as you are, but you can teach a number of shortcuts which most homemakers will appreciate.

The use of specially shaped pans is great for beginners. There are lambs and bunnies and hearts and now Wilton has a collection of Disney-character pans.

There are a number of easy decorating tricks you can teach your students. One of our favorites is the transfer. It's quite simple but very effective.

Take a birthday napkin, or any picture with an appropriate design—for example, a clown face. Cut out the design and trace it onto a piece of waxed paper.

Cut out the waxed-paper outline and transfer it onto the frosted cake. Tap the edge of the outline lightly with a toothpick, and then carefully peel the paper off. You will then have the outline impressed on the cake as a guide and you can fill in with appropriate colors using a small star tip. One woman who used this method cut an animal design from one of the birthday napkins she was using for her son's party and transferred it to the cake as described above, matching the colors as closely as possible. This gave the table an attractive, coordinated look. You could offer to do this as part of your unique service.

All kinds of clever ideas can be used by the "cut-out" decorating method, starting with the standard round, square, and rectangular cake pans. You will find ideas in magazines, especially around holiday time. Some of our best ideas on cut-out cakes have come from *Baker's Cut-Up Cake Party Book,* which is published as a premium by General Foods Company.

We've also found that the following Carousel Cake is a favorite for a child's birthday party. Start off with two 8″ round layer cake pans, a paper-towel tube, four straws, and a paper doily.

Directions: Bake and frost smoothly an 8″ layer cake, making sure to level off any uneven mounds before frosting. Cut about 1½″ off the end of the paper-towel tube and discard the smaller piece. Frost only the portion of the remaining tube that will show when placed in the cake. To do this, center it in the middle of the cake and carefully push it down. This will provide the center "post" for the carousel. You can further decorate this post by piping diagonal lines starting at the top of it and coming down at a slight angle until you reach the bottom. Repeat this procedure a few more times until the piping effect looks complete. Then, for the finishing touch to the post, add some small flowers on the piping at spaced intervals.

Push the straws upright into the cake, near the edge, in four spots equidistant from each other. For the carousel "top," place the lace doily centered on the decorated paper-towel tube, and attach the edges or corners to each straw, using a dab of frosting as "glue," if needed, to hold it in place.

Use your imagination for the carousel "figures." You can buy plastic horses, ballerinas, and so forth at a cake-decorating store, or use animal crackers which would be edible, too. You could even outline the crackers with colorful frosting to dress them up a bit.

A ROADSIDE MARKET CAN BE A MONEY MAKER

In spite of the convenience of superhighways, many drivers still prefer to travel on scenic back roads where they can stop to browse, buy local produce, or find a snack.

A roadside stand is an ideal way to provide simple but good food to hungry travelers and to sell items you make or produce you grow.

Roadside stands featuring homemade ice cream are particularly popular, especially in resort areas such as beaches, state parks, camping grounds, and so on. These roads are usually well traveled and most people are eager to stop for something refreshing.

As far as we can gather the first man to sample a frozen dessert was Nero, the emperor of Rome. The story goes that he had his subjects gather snow on the mountains and rush back to the palace, whereupon he mixed it with fruit juices and flavorings, coming up with an older version of our popular water ice. Even today, some of the best sellers are very simple but mouthwatering refreshments and desserts.

One family that lived across the street from a beach capitalized on its especially good hot fudge sauce by selling sundaes and also packaging the syrup in individual pint and quart containers to be bought and taken home. No doubt there are thousands of similar family enterprises such as this, not necessarily limited to the sale of ice cream and cold refreshments. Other possibilities include homemade candy, steamed hot dogs, clams, fresh buttered popcorn, as well as caramels, taffy apples, or whatever kitchen concoction you have to offer. Use your imagination and don't be afraid to try. Sometimes what may often be dismissed as a ridiculously simple product will go over in a big way, depending on the location of your stand, the time of year, and the appeal of buying something reasonably priced that really hits the spot.

Spring, summer, and autumn are the most likely times when people will be traveling the scenic routes. But don't rule out winter if you happen to live on a road leading to or near a ski resort. A roadside stand offering hot coffee, hot chocolate, sandwiches, homemade pie, brownies, or cookies could bring you a healthy extra income. Again, it's up to you to use your judgment in determining the possibilities that exist for what you

124

wish to offer, taking into consideration how heavily traveled your road is and how convenient the location of your stand. If space permits, it is a nice idea to have some picnic tables and benches set up so travelers can sit down for a bit and enjoy the scenery when the weather is pleasant.

If you grow your own vegetables, a roadside stand is a great way to make the most of your gardening efforts. And, of course, at Hallowe'en time pumpkins are much in demand. If you have a talent for making pretty arrangements out of dried flowers, pods, and all the natural resources on hand, by all means display some of your creations along with your produce. Make the most of your opportunities and talents!

YOU'VE GOT IT MADE IF YOU GO AFTER THE SCHOOL-LUNCH TRADE

Most schools today are eligible for federally subsidized hot lunches through the National School Lunch Program initiated in 1946. Yet many schools still do not have the facilities that would enable them to offer a hot-lunch program to their students. Some of these schools are in low-income districts, but many others are located in average- or above-average-income areas that are without lunchrooms. Among these are schools for the handicapped, religious schools, small private schools, and even some public schools. Parents are required to pack lunches for their children or else let them eat lunch at nearby fast-food chains which offer little in the way of variety, less by way of nutrition.

If you live near a school that does not have the facilities to offer a hot-lunch program, here is an opportunity for you to offer your own private lunch program. This has been done quite successfully by some enterprising women who realized that they could offer a very worthwhile service to some children (and grateful mothers) while supplementing their own incomes.

Before initiating such a program, be sure to check with your local zoning board to see if this type of service would be allowed, particularly if you live in a residentially zoned area. It may be necessary for you to obtain a variance. Once you have cleared it with the zoning board, your next step would be to contact your local health department. Your facilities will have to be inspected by a health officer before you receive a license, and a medical check-up for you will be necessary. You may possibly have to apply for a foster day-care license from your State Department of Children and Family Services.

Prior to doing this, it would be advisable for you to acquaint yourself with the "Type-A" School Lunch, which is the nutritional pattern set by the U. S. Department of Agriculture. It is planned to provide approximately one-third of the daily nutritional requirements of a student ten to twelve years of age. You can make necessary adjustments in suggested portions depending on the ages of the children to whom you are providing your service. To obtain information on this plan, write to: Superintendent of Documents, U. S. Government Printing Office, Washington, D. C. 20402, requesting their leaflet entitled *A Menu Planning Guide for Type-A*

School Lunches (PA-719), U. S. Department of Agriculture Consumer and Marketing Service. This is offered to schools participating in the National School Lunch Program but would also be informative to those interested in starting their own private service.

To provide this service, you need a room and facilities large enough to hold at least a dozen children. A large dining room, family room, or finished basement equipped with picnic benches or individual card tables and chairs would be adequate. You may need an oven apart from the one used for your regular family cooking to be used specifically in preparing your lunches. (Again, the health department will fill you in on such matters.) Sturdy plastic dishes and utensils and plastic placemats could be used to cut down on maintenance. Once you have met all the requirements and obtained the necessary equipment, a few calls to mothers of school children in your area should be sufficient to get your business underway. Make up some flyers with some sample menus to send them so they will be assured that their children will be getting nutritious and appetizing meals.

CARE PACKAGES FOR THE COLLEGE CROWD: A PART-TIME BUSINESS THAT PAYS OFF

If you live near a college, an academy, or a private boarding school, a special opportunity exists!

Mail parents a flyer offering to deli'er a special, food-energy package during exam weeks. This is a time when students who are busy cramming for exams are likely to skip meals and cram whatever is handy into their mouths. This usually consists of anything edible that comes out of a machine. An alternative is a special food-energy package delivered by you during exam weeks.

It could be packaged in a carton with a gummed label marked CARE PACKAGE *from someone who* DOES CARE! Under this the name of the parent or parents could be included. This idea already has a success record at dozens of schools.

Your package will contain nourishing as well as

energy-producing snacks such as fresh fruit, dry roasted nuts, a cheese ball or log, along with some good crackers, an assortment of cut-up raw vegetables with a special dip, some cold salads including potato salad, chicken or ham salad, a three-bean salad or carrot-raisin salad, and, *very important,* instructions to the kids about *refrigeration.* Anything with mayonnaise, for instance, MUST be refrigerated. And, of course, provide some standard but always welcome treats such as homemade brownies, chocolate-chip or oatmeal cookies, and fudge. These are usually fast-energy favorites among the snack-happy younger set.

Here are some recipes that will give you an idea of what the college crowd enjoys:

GOOD-FOR-YOU COOKIES

⅔ cup molasses
⅓ cup oil
1 cup squash or
   sweet potatoes,
   cooked
2 eggs
½ cup wheat germ
   (or oatmeal)
½ cup wheat flour

¾ cup white flour
1 cup powdered milk
½ cup brown sugar
1 to 1½ cups raisins
1 tsp. salt
1 tsp. cinnamon
½ tsp. nutmeg
½ tsp. ginger

Mix everything but the raisins in a bowl until well blended. Then stir in the raisins. Add wheat germ or oatmeal, if necessary, so that cookie batter will not spread out when teaspoonsful are dropped on greased cookie sheet. Bake at 350° for 10 to 15 minutes. Store in refrigerator.

CARROT CAKE

3 cups sifted flour
2 tsps. baking powder
1½ tsps. baking soda
2 tsps. cinnamon

1 cup cooking oil
1½ cups sugar
4 whole eggs
2 cups grated carrots
1 cup chopped nuts

Sift first four ingredients together. Add the rest of the ingredients. Bake for 1¼ hours at 300°. Press top with finger, lightly. If cake is done, it springs back. You can use an angelfood pan or a 13″ x 9″ x 2″ pan.

CREAM CHEESE FROSTING

One 8-ounce pkg. cream cheese
½ to 1 stick margarine
1-pound box sifted confectioners' sugar
dash salt
2 tsps. vanilla

Cream together cream cheese and margarine. Add remaining ingredients, blending thoroughly. Frost carrot cake.

ENERGY CANDY

¼ cup molasses
¼ cup honey
½ cup peanut butter

1 cup powdered milk
½ cup seedless raisins

Mix all ingredients well in bowl and form a ball. Add more powdered milk if necessary. Knead until stiff. Cut into small squares and roll in brown sugar if desired. Let stand for a couple of hours until hardened. Be sure to use *powdered* milk, not crystalline dry milk.

MOLASSES GINGER SNAPS

¾ cup margarine or shortening	1 tsp. baking soda
	¼ tsp. salt
1 cup sugar	1 tsp. cinnamon
¼ cup molasses	1 tsp. cloves
1 egg	1 tsp. ginger
2 cups flour	

Mix together all the ingredients. Form into balls. Roll in sugar. Place wide apart on slightly greased cookie sheet. Bake at 375° for 8 to 10 minutes. Makes 3 to 4 dozen.

BEAN
SALAD

1 can cut green
  beans
1 can wax beans
1 can red kidney
  beans
1 small green
  pepper, chopped
1 small onion,
  chopped

3 tbls. sugar
1 tsp. salt
1 tsp. pepper
½ cup red-wine
  vinegar
½ cup salad oil
1 purple onion
  (for garnish)

Drain liquid from beans and discard. Mix well all other ingredients, and marinate vegetables at least 8 hours. Give beans a stir now and then. Salad may be garnished with sliced purple onion.

CARROT
RAISIN
SALAD

2 cups grated carrots
1 cup raisins (seedless)
*½ cup flaked coconut or 2 finely
  grated apples*

Combine with mayonnaise to taste. Refrigerate.

BEST
CHICKEN
SALAD

*2–3 cups chopped
  cooked chicken*
1 tbls. minced onion
1 tsp. salt
2 tbls. lemon juice
*1 cup chopped
  celery*

*1 cup drained, cut
  pineapple*
*½ cup toasted
  almonds*
Mayonnaise to taste

Combine chicken, onion, salt, lemon juice and celery. Refrigerate several hours. Fold in pineapple, almonds, and mayonnaise when ready to serve.

PERFECT POTATO SALAD

2½ cups cooked, diced potatoes
1 tsp. sugar
1 tsp. vinegar
½ cup chopped onion
1½ tsp. salt

½ cup sliced celery
¼ cup sliced sweet pickles (optional)
¾ cup mayonnaise
2 hard-cooked eggs, sliced

Sprinkle potatoes with sugar and vinegar. Add onion, celery, sweet pickles, salt, and mayonnaise; toss to blend. Carefully fold in eggs. May be garnished with parsley, paprika, sliced radishes, cucumbers or egg slices. Refrigerate.

1-2-3
DIP

1 cup dairy sour cream
½ envelope cheese-garlic-flavored salad
  dressing mix
¼ tsp. salt
Few drops bottled hot pepper sauce

Combine ingredients. Serve with raw vegetables. Keep chilled.

A TISKET, A TASKET:
PEOPLE LOVE RECEIVING A
SPECIAL-OCCASION BASKET

Preparing baskets full of goodies as gifts for special occasions can develop into a very good business. Gift baskets are great for saying, "Happy Birthday," or *"Bon Voyage,"* or "Get Well," or "Happy Holiday." It's a business you can start anywhere.

One good example of putting this idea to work is a Vermont mother who was widowed and left with three children to support. She wanted to earn money enough to raise her children without taking on an outside job. She had always done her own preserving for her family and decided to capitalize on this. So she set a goal for herself to put up 400 jars a day (yes, 400!), with the assistance of her children. She arranged to purchase cheeses and pure Vermont maple syrup from local merchants at wholesale prices, since she would be purchasing in quantity. She packaged her homemade preserves, the cheese, and pure maple syrup in attractive baskets tied with calico bows. Her next step was to contact businessmen in the area with a "sampler," suggesting they purchase these baskets as company Christmas gifts that the whole family could enjoy. Received enthusiastically, these Christmas baskets earned our novice businesswoman a seasonal income of from $6,000 to $7,000. But her sales were not by any means limited to the Christmas season. Local gift shops displayed her samplers year round and for several years she was able to support her family working right from her kitchen as she had hoped to do.

It would be simple to develop gift packages that you can market for birthdays, Mother's Day, *bon voyage* presents, and get-well remembrances as an alternative to the usual flowers. In fact, there is hardly an occasion when this type of gift would not be happily received and appropriate. Do be careful about the healthful contents of get-well baskets.

Your gift baskets need not be limited to food only. Other special touches and remembrances could be included, depending on the occasion and the personal interests of the recipient. Offer special de luxe packages with useful items. For instance a housewarming basket might include small cooking utensils, pot holders, a cookbook, or pretty dish towels. Stationery and greeting cards could be welcome in a get-well package.

Other items that might be welcome in baskets are

decorative recipe cards, appointment books, memo pads, and calendars. At Thanksgiving or Christmas a pretty calendar for the coming year would be appropriate. Your gift baskets can be as personalized as you and the client wish to make it. If you enjoy shopping around and picking out just the right gift, you could offer this as part of your service to prospective customers. Some women have started very successful businesses as shoppers for busy executives who don't have the time to shop themselves. Just be sure to establish price guidelines beforehand, so you won't be stuck with an unusual gift item that is out of the price range of the client. If you are lucky enough to purchase an item at a sale or special discount, you may feel perfectly justified in charging the customer the full retail price of the item. Remember, you are the one putting in your time, energy, and imagination. And you must calculate how to charge for your time in addition.

CANDY IS DANDY
FOR MAKING MONEY

Fancy boxes notwithstanding, production-line chocolates never have the appeal that homemade or hand-dipped candy has. Just the word "homemade" fills our heads with visions of sweets that are richer, nuttier, more chocolate, more delicious than any that come packaged.

There are three essentials to keep in mind in producing superior candy—reliable, kitchen-tested recipes, an *accurate* candy thermometer, and good ingredients.

Good recipes are plentiful. Cookbooks are filled with them. At holiday times, popular magazines are good sources. Most libraries usually carry several time-honored cookbooks on the art of candy making.

An accurate candy thermometer is needed to ensure

success in candy making. Most reliable sources recommend checking your new candy thermometer for accuracy by placing it in a pan of water and bringing the water to a boiling point (212° F.). Your thermometer should register at the boiling point. If it doesn't, attach a tag indicating the correct boiling point on your gauge so that all other temperatures can be calculated accordingly, or get a better thermometer. The Taylor Candy-Jelly-Frosting thermometer costs about $3.50 and is excellent. Never use a dial-type or oven thermometer. These are not accurate enough for candy making.

If you want to produce candy that is really superior in quality, this is one area where it never pays to skimp by replacing a rich ingredient with one that is cheaper but also less palatable. Some sweets can tolerate this, but candy is not one of them. For instance, there is nothing like real, honest-to-goodness rich cream for making superior caramels. And in marketing something like candy, your product has to be a standout.

There are many different and delicious types of candy you can make, such as fudge, caramels, toffee, fondant, peanut clusters, brittle, hard candies, fruit and mint jellies, nougat, divinity, marzipan, and several buttercream fillings for chocolates.

While it was once true that making chocolates was better left to the commercial experts, this is no longer the case. With all the aids available now, often through cake-decorating stores, you can turn out professional-looking confections in a relatively easy, fun, and profitable way. All kinds of special candy molds can be purchased in novel shapes such as peanuts, pumpkins, flowers, leaves, umbrellas, baby dolls, as well as holiday designs. There is even a "continental" tray which will enable you to make very elegant-looking chocolates such as you see in expensive candy stores. Just about everything you can think of for authentic candy making is available, including quality bulk chocolate for chipping and melting down and materials that will enable you to package your candy in a professional-looking way. These include the small fluted paper or foil cups used by commercial candy makers and attractive gift boxes with a special label, "From the kitchen of ———," on the cover. You could become the 1970s answer to Fannie Farmer!

One woman in Connecticut is making quite a career for herself by demonstrating candy-making techniques using professionally designed molds. Her husband is a photographer who works at cake shows that feature all the latest techniques and ideas in cake decorating. He then travels upon request to various cake-decorating clubs, showing slides of these creations. Now his wife joins him and adds to the evening's information by demonstrating her candy making as well.

If these supplies are not available at your local cake-decorating or department stores, you can write to the address below for information about obtaining candy-making equipment. Also, a booklet is available for $1.25 entitled *How to Mold Fancy Candy and Sugar*. It also contains special candy recipes. We highly recommend sending for this booklet. Write to:

Candy & Cake Craft Company
31 Mildred Road
West Hartford, Conn. 06107

Once you have mastered the art of producing superior homemade candy, how do you profit from it? First of all, reread the chapter on pricing at the beginning of this book and make sure that all items of cost and expense are taken into account when you price your product. Candy made in your kitchen is a product that should fetch a premium price compared to commercially produced candy.

However, while you can and should receive "top dollar" for your candy, remember that the prices you charge cannot be so far above those charged by a commercial producer that your potential customers will be forced to pass up your product. Before setting your prices, shop around and find out what your commercial competitors are charging in the localities where you plan to sell your candy. Notice how their products are packaged. This may give you ideas for improving your competitive advantage. For example, if a store is charging $1.60 for a pound of fudge that is packaged in a dull cardboard box, you could display your fudge in an attractive box and you could add a small ribbon or other distinctively designed decoration. Now, together with your homemade quality, this may enable you successfully to market your fudge at $2.25 a pound, well above $1.60. Thus you receive "top dollar" with minimal extra expense.

144

Speaking of marketing, how *do* you market your candy now that you have attractively packaged and priced it? First, be sure to take advantage of inexpensive local advertising sources such as newspapers, school and church bulletin boards, and so on. Also, approach local merchants and persuade them to stock your product. We are not necessarily thinking about a giant supermarket; a much better prospect may be a specialty store such as a cheese shop or even a florist. This is where you can use your ingenuity and enthusiasm to convince these merchants that this arrangement will also increase *their* business. After all, candy and flowers go together like love and marriage! As an added inducement, you could agree to give the merchant 10 percent of each sale for his efforts.

Another way to build your candy business is to give free candy-making demonstrations at various club meetings. This will increase appreciation of and desire for homemade candy in your community. Don't be concerned about creating future competitors; these clubwomen are primarily interested in enjoying good candy and knowing something about making it. They are not prepared to make the commitment you have made in starting and building your own business.

Another idea would be to give classes at a candy-making school in your own kitchen (see page 68 on establishing a cooking school). This would tend to validate your reputation as an expert in candy making, bring in extra money from instruction fees, and build your candy sales all in one fell swoop.

145

Here are some recipes you may enjoy:

CHERRY
VANILLA
FUDGE

3 cups sugar
½ tsp. salt
1 cup light cream
½ cup milk
¼ cup light corn
  syrup

2 tbls. butter
2 tsps. vanilla
1 cup red and green
  candied cherries,
  quartered

Combine sugar, salt, cream, milk, corn syrup, and butter in a large, heavy saucepan. Cook over medium heat, stirring constantly, until mixture comes to a boil. Continue cooking, stirring occasionally, until candy thermometer reaches 238° (soft-ball stage). Remove from heat, leaving thermometer in saucepan. Cool to 100°. Add vanilla, beat briskly until fudge thickens and begins to lose its gloss. Stir in cherries. Pour into 8″ square buttered pan. Cool. Cut into squares when firm.

PINK
PEPPERMINT
PATTIES

1 pkg. (1 lb.) confectioners' sugar
3 tbls. light corn syrup
3 tbls. water
½ tsp. peppermint extract
Red food coloring
Royal Frosting (recipe follows)

Combine confectioners' sugar, corn syrup, and water in top of double boiler. Heat over simmering water (do not allow water to boil or steam—will dull the tops of shiny patties), stirring several times, until sugar dissolves and mixture is smooth. Remove from heat, but let mixture stand over hot water to keep soft for shaping. Stir in peppermint extract.

To make white candies, drop half of mixture, a teaspoonful at a time, onto cookie sheets to form 1″ rounds. Let stand until firm.

To tint candies, stir a few drops of red food coloring into remaining mixture in top of

147

double boiler, then shape, following directions as above. Let stand until firm.

Decorate each with a dainty leaf or flower
design, using Royal Frosting.

ROYAL
FROSTING

2 egg whites
1 tsp. lemon juice
3½ cups sifted confectioners' sugar

Beat egg whites with lemon juice in a me-
dium-size mixing bowl until foamy white. Add
confectioners' sugar gradually, beating until
frosting stands in firm peaks and is stiff
enough to hold a sharp line when cut through
with a knife.

OLD-TIME
FUDGE

3 cups sugar
1 cup milk
Three 1-ounce squares unsweetened
  chocolate
Dash salt
2 tsps. corn syrup, light or dark
3 tbls. butter
1½ tsps. vanilla

Butter sides of heavy 3-qt. saucepan. In it combine sugar, milk, chocolate, salt, and corn syrup. Heat over medium heat, stirring constantly till sugar dissolves, chocolate melts, and mixture comes to a boil. Then cook to soft-ball stage (234°), stirring only if necessary. Immediately remove from heat; add butter and cool to lukewarm (110°) without stirring. Add vanilla. Beat vigorously until fudge becomes very thick and starts to lose its gloss. Quickly spread in buttered shallow pan or small platter. Score in squares while

149

warm and, if desired, top each with a walnut half; cut when firm.

Note: If you like, quickly stir in ½ cup broken nuts at end of beating time when fudge begins to lose its gloss.

ROCKY ROAD

Four 4½-ounce milk-chocolate bars
3 cups miniature marshmallows
¾ cup coarsely broken walnuts

Partially melt chocolate over hot water; remove from heat and beat until smooth. Stir in marshmallows and nuts. Spread in buttered 8″ pan. Chill until firm. Cut in squares.

CHOCOLATE
AND
ALMOND
TOFFEE

1 lb. butter
2½ cups sugar
Two 3½-ounce cans blanched, sliced
* almonds (about 2 cups)*
Eight 1-ounce squares semisweet chocolate
Two 4-ounce bars sweet cooking chocolate
* (German's chocolate)*

Lightly butter a 15½ x 10½ x 1-inch baking pan. In a large, heavy saucepan combine the 1 lb. butter and the sugar. Place over moderate heat. Bring mixture to full boil, stirring to blend well. Cover tightly and cook three minutes.

Uncover and continue to cook 5 to 10 minutes, stirring occasionally, until candy thermometer registers 290° F. Quickly pour mixture into prepared pan. Refrigerate until toffee is firm, about 15 minutes.

Meanwhile, to toast almonds, heat oven to 300°. Place almonds in shallow pan and bake 10 to 15 minutes or until lightly browned, stirring occasionally.

Put 4 squares of semisweet chocolate and 1 bar sweet chocolate in top of double boiler over hot water. Heat until chocolate is melted, stirring until blended smooth. Spread the melted chocolate over the toffee and sprinkle with half of the almonds. Return to refrigerator until chocolate is set, 30 to 45 minutes. Meanwhile melt remaining chocolate over hot water. Invert toffee onto a sheet of aluminum foil. Spread the second side of the toffee with the remaining melted chocolate, and sprinkle with remaining almonds. Refrigerate until chocolate is set. With the point of a heavy-duty knife, break candy into bite-size pieces. Makes about 3 lbs.

Part III

THE KITCHEN CRAFT SPECIALIST

Gold in your kitchen; how to make money in your kitchen. The idea is intriguing, but, and it's a big but, preparing and cooking food for a business is not all that appealing to *you*.

You're really more into creating, into doing things with your hands. You find making something to use, or wear, or appreciate is more stimulating and you always come up with new ideas.

Then, you can still put that imagination and creativity to work in your kitchen to start a small crafts business that will bring in extra income as well as extra enjoyment.

After all, what is nicer than doing something you like to do and getting paid for it.

TURN "GARBAGE" INTO GREEN GOLD: PLANT IT

Stop. Before you throw away those avocado pits, carrot tops, citrus seeds, and other "kitchen waste," give a thought to the fact that this could be the stuff upon which a profitable business could grow. All it takes is a little imagination and even less investment, and you can turn your kitchen "garbage" into a nicely growing plant business that you can both enjoy and profit from.

Plants are big business. And, if you shop for something a bit more exotic than the common philodendron, you'll find out just how expensive a plant can be. Still, plants are favorites for decorating apartments and houses; good gifts for saying "Happy Birthday" or *"Bon Voyage"* or "Thank You," and perfect for housewarming, hostess, or hospital gifts. Plants are the kind of gift a child can give to a teacher or a friend can give to a neighbor that will be welcomed and appreciated for years.

Not only can you rescue these plants from the garbage, but you can save cans and bottles and turn those into attractive planters to help you set a good price for the final product.

Selling your plants calls for some research if you want to make your name beyond your neighborhood. Check out neighborhood, church, school, and charity bazaars and fairs. Place a small ad in your local newspaper or weekly shopper. Send out flyers to all your friends and neighbors.

You might want to contact people who are planning a garage sale and offer to set up a plant stand at their sale offering them a percentage of the profits. Don't ignore small local shops such as the gift, book, or grocer's shop that might be willing to take in a selection on consignment.

The most marvelous thing about garbage gardening is that these plants you grow are unique—usually not available at commercial florists—which makes them great for gifts. (One of the drawbacks is that some of the plants won't last more than a few seasons before they die or need to be transferred to an outdoor garden.)

But, as we pointed out, the investment is small. You'll need containers or pots, but along with clay pots you can use the other usual candidates for the garbage—tin cans and jars. The cans (coffee cans are particularly good) should be punched with small holes in the bottom for drainage. Before filling with soil, line the bottom of the pot with stones or pieces of broken china or clay pot. This also helps with drainage.

Seeds germinate best in a sterile medium. It's best to use one of the commercial packaged "starter mixes" which may be obtained at a local plant nursery. Some of the better known ones are Vermiculite, Terralite, Perlite, and milled sphagnum. Packaged soil is also sterile, but you should probably add clean sand or peat to it for drainage.

Commercially available peat pots are also convenient to use as seed starters because the peat, with the sprouted seedling, can be transplanted with less shock to the plant than by other methods.

Here are some of the plants that you can grow easily.

THE AVOCADO

(Persea Americana)

Avocado plants have their own cult. Avocado-plant owners actually have beauty contests for their pet plants. These plants are not only easy to start but they are hardy and great for office decoration since they flourish under fluorescent lights.

To grow an avocado plant, wash and dry the pit. Peel away the papery-thin pit covering. Fill a jar with water and suspend the pit in water, using toothpicks or long thin metal pins. Don't worry that the pins or picks will do any damage. They go into the pit about a quarter of an inch and all the action takes place in the center. The pit should be about half in water, broadest base downward. Roots will appear in several weeks and then the pit can be planted in soil. Avocados need good drainage. They also need to be clipped to encourage side branching. Staking the plant will also keep it attractive. Advise buyers to clip and repot from time to time and their avocado will, with care, grow into a handsome indoor tree.

THE CITRUS TREE

A grapefruit or orange tree that you grow from seed yourself will probably never bear fruit but with care and sunshine it will blossom. You can start six to eight seeds in an 8″ or 10″ pot. First line the bottom with potsherds then fill with soil. A good mixture is one-third potting soil, one-third sand, and one-third peat moss. Add some dried manure available from your local nursery. Soak, mix well. Drain out excess water and push seeds down about ¼″ to ½″, allowing ample space between each seed. Keep your citrus plants in the sunniest spot you can find at a temperature above 65° If the sun fails you, try a plant light or a 100-watt bulb directly above the pot at least 2′ from the tips of the leaves.

The trick to growing citrus plants is at least four hours of light each day and keeping the soil evenly moist. Avoid allowing it to become either soggy or dry.

The first lovely green sprouts should shoot up in about three or four weeks. In a few months, transfer into individual pots using the same soil mix. Instruct purchasers that citrus plants must have light and must be kept moist.

THE CARROT

Lovely plants with light and feathery green leaves grow from carrot tops. Cut 3″ to 4″ pieces from the tops of the freshest carrots you can buy and place cut ends down in a shallow container covered half-way with water. Maintain the water level. When a sizable number of new leaves sprout from the top, transplant each new plant to an individual pot using a regular potting-soil mix.

THE DATE PALM
(Phoenix Dactylifera)

You need those luscious, rich natural dates available at health-food and Middle Eastern stores. Steamed and pasteurized ones won't do. Enjoy the sweet tender meat of your dates; then wash the pits, put them in a starter mix and wait. Date palm germination could be as long as two months or more. Keep your containers in a warm place and cover the plant to keep humid. A good investment is a table greenhouse with heating cables in the bottom which ensures even temperatures for your plants. Otherwise prop plastic on sticks to create your own "greenhouse." With the date pit, the growth will be coming from below the ground, pushing its way through the soil slowly. When growth reaches 1" above the soil, transplant into a tub of rich soil. The growth will be joined by a second one, and eventually the fronds will appear. Date palms need light, moisture, and nourishment. They grow into beautiful and exotic indoor trees.

THE PEPPER PLANT

Flowering pepper plants can be grown from fresh hot red-pepper seeds like the kind so many of us keep dried on our spice shelves. The seeds must be whole, not ground, and fresh. You plant eight to ten seeds in a 5" pot in a rich moist soil. Cover with about ¼" of starter mix. Water lightly and place in a table greenhouse or under plastic. Keep soil moist but not soaked and mist daily after plants begin to grow. Advise your customers to feed pepper plants regularly and keep in warm fresh air. Plants will bloom with tiny white flowers that will develop into pods—at first white, then yellow, then red. Withering peppers should be picked to keep continuing fruiting.

SWEET POTATO PLANTS

These plants are rare these days because of the common practice of kiln drying to give sweet potatoes longer shelf life. For your business, take a trip to the farmer's market and look for potatoes with live sprouts. All it takes to grow a sweet potato plant is water, warmth, and sun. Suspend your sweet potatoes in a jar, large end up with the bottom half covered with water. Vines start within a few weeks. Never let plant dry out; add plant food but at approximately one-half the recommended strength. When the sweet potato is blooming, make cuttings and root in water or peat. Never pot the sweet potato itself. Your permanent plants will come from the cuttings.

THE PINEAPPLE

(Ananas Comosus)

The leafy pineapple is a favorite with many plant lovers. For pineapple plants you slash off the crown about 1″ below the base of the leaves. Scrape out the fruity section and air-dry for a day or two. Place the pineapple crown in a dish of peat moss. When a healthy growth of roots appears it's time to pot. Pineapples need good drainage, so remember to put potsherds in the bottom of the pot. Try a mix of one-half potting soil and one-half sand and give these plants plenty of sunlight and

161

warmth. Advise buyers to spray leaves with a mister a few times each week.

POMEGRANATE PLANT

(Punica granatum)

Most of us when eating a pomegranate feel that there is more seed than fruit. So, make the seeds pay off. Rinse away the fleshy part from the seeds and allow to dry a few days. To germinate, place the seeds in shallow pans of sterile mix and cover with table greenhouse or plastic. Mold will probably accumulate on the seed but this is part of the germination process. In about eight to ten weeks, growth should begin. Transplant seedlings to individual pots. Pomegranates need a rich soil—a mix of potting soil and humus. In transplanting, the seed and tap root should be completely covered. Lovely leaves should appear in just a few weeks. The pomegranate thrives on warmth and sun. Soil should be kept evenly moist but high humidity should be avoided.

OTHER EXOTIC PLANTS

You can grow beautiful plants and trees from mangoes, guavas, litchi nuts, papaya, passion fruit, persimmon, coconuts, and dozens of other fruits and vegetables.

162

There are many books on growing plants and before starting even the most casual of operations you should research the subject. (See Bibliography.) Plants have varying periods of germination. For example, it takes a year before a coconut plant looks like a palm tree. It might sell for an attractive sum but in the same amount of time you could have grown and sold dozens of avocado or citrus plants which do not have to be fully grown to go on the market.

Growing plants also takes space and sunlight. When your business takes off, you might want to invest in a lean-to greenhouse. Your plant business may never evolve into a big commercial operation. You probably wouldn't want it to grow too large, but if you have a green thumb and love plants it can be a very pleasant way of adding to your income.

Packaging can add to your plant profits. If plants are big business, planters are just as big. Since your plants come from the fruits and vegetables of the kitchen, be imaginative and plant them in the bottles, jars, cartons, and tin cans you would ordinarily throw away. Women's magazines are always full of ideas and from there you can let your imagination take off. We've seen squat, wide-mouth jars wired together with hangers in clusters of three or four and made into attractive hanging planters, cardboard milk cartons cut and decorated to look like ships or houses made into holders for carrying away small plants.

A KNACK WITH DOUGH CAN BRING IN LOTS OF BREAD

A very elegant boutique on Madison Avenue in New York charges somewhat exorbitant prices for decorative items made from dough. One of them is nothing more than a beautifully twisted loaf of bread.

We've also seen bread and fruit baskets made of dough selling at high prices. If you have the kind of imagination that can turn the most ordinary of substances from the kitchen into something that someone will be willing to pay for, then dough creations might be just the bread business to go into for big profits.

Most of the dough recipes are made with flour, salt, and water with vegetables or even instant tea for coloring. Other materials: paint, varnish, shellac, acrylic sealer, epoxy cement, hooks for hanging.

As for the tools, kitchenware, cookie sheets, cutters,

molds, toothpicks, wax paper, and aluminum foil are all that are necessary, though as a professional, you might prefer to buy and use clay modeling tools.

With the prices of basic materials so low, the biggest consideration in cost will be your creativity and talent.

The mechanics of making bread sculpture are simple. Basic recipes abound. One excellent mixture calls for 2 cups flour, 1 cup salt, 1 cup warm water with 1 teaspoon instant tea added to the water for the baked-bread color.

You can also bake your creations or let them air dry. Some boutiques have made a selling point of the fact that the sculptures are not baked but are long-lasting. It really doesn't make a difference in the product, but somehow the statement seems to have consumer appeal.

Unbaked dough, unless colored, will result in white sculptures which are best for painting. You can also add a vegetable coloring in the water for the dough or you can knead a coloring in to get a marbleized effect.

To start your business you can find a wealth of ideas in back issues of women's magazines and craft books, and one of the best instruction books we've seen is *The Dough-It-Yourself Handbook,* which Morton Salt sells as a premium for $1.00.

In this book you'll find instruction for making bread baskets, cachepots, small serving dishes, all of which seem to be most salable if my study of what is on sale in retail stores is an indication.

Beautifully twisted bread loaves, croissants, and rolls

complete with hooks for hanging also seem to be favored as kitchen decorations.

Christmas decorations are popular, too, and one of our dough favorites is a beautiful *Della Robbia*-like wreath of warm golden-brown fruit and nuts, leaves, and ribbons all individually sculpted and glued to a flat, round base.

If you feel your free-form artistic talent is somewhat less than professional, don't despair. You can still make lovely creations using molds and cookie cutters.

Dough is also a flexible medium. In addition to the objects we've already mentioned, we've seen jewelry, floral arrangements, decorative wall plaques, frames for pictures and mirrors, toys and doll-house furniture, all made from dough.

Indulge yourself and experiment before you decide which product or products you want to sell. If the products you create are highly professional looking, you can try to sell them through the finest retail stores in town. Dough creations are unique gifts and it appears that consumers are prepared to pay a premium price for an item that is as useful as it is unusual.

WHAT PRICE FOR AN EGGSHELL? IT DEPENDS ON YOU

The enameled eggs by Fabergé, made for the czars of Russia, are museum objects. Why not? The egg itself is a form of enduring beauty which artists and craftsmen through the ages have recognized and sought to enhance. Exquisitely decorated eggs make memorable gifts for Easter, Valentine's Day, birthdays, weddings, as Christmas ornaments, or as fragile, beautiful gifts at any time.

We've owned eggs of every type. Among our favorites were a hinged and jeweled replica of a Fabergé creation, and a beautiful, hand-painted work of modern art.

There are dozens of ways to decorate eggs. There are Far-Eastern designs, lace eggs, découpage eggs, batik eggs, eggs with Christmas scenes inserted, the Ukrainian *Pysanky* eggs.

167

Do your own thing . . . or look for ideas in craft books and consumer magazines.

Where you sell your creations depends on what kind of eggs you choose to make. The Fabergé models would do well in gift boutiques, possibly even in jewelry stores. Candy stores, bakeries, and other food shops are good outlets for your hand-painted eggs. Bookstores, card shops, and other specialized shops are also possible outlets for your products.

We've also come across a craftswoman who creates beautiful still lifes of eggshell mosaics. The shells are dyed in vibrant colors with fabric dyes, broken into tiny pieces and applied to your background drawing in the proper areas. To apply, cover back of eggshell with glue, apply to painting, and press flat. The pressure will produce a cracked, mosaic-like effect. Finish the piece by spraying with clear Krylon finish.

PASTA IS PERFECT
FOR A
PROFITABLE BUSINESS

A craftswoman we know used to live by the oceanside when she was a little girl, and like most of the children she knew she collected shells. However, when they made shell jewelry, they often ignored the real things and raided their mothers' pantry shelves for pasta! Pasta shells were so easy to work with, to thread together, to glue. They left the shells natural or painted them in bright colors or gilded them. They used shells of one size or mixed sizes and varieties together.

They thought pasta shells were very beautiful then and surprisingly more and more people are finding pasta perfect for decorating objects today. It seems that in this ecologically oriented world the combination of beauty and biodegradable is good for sales.

169

Moreover, consumers are always looking for something different and it seems that the "natural" look will be with us for a while, giving objects such as mirrors, cachepots, boxes, and frames made with pasta a decorative cachet.

Naturally, if you want to go into business, your products will have to have a more finished appearance than the "loving-hands-at-home" look of most kitchen-craft items.

Let's assume that you're both creative and craftsmanlike in your approach to this business and that you'd rather whip together a decorator's delight than a delicious dish made from pasta. But, how much is that talent worth?

It depends on your flair, your taste, your inventiveness. Your ability to produce professional-looking products makes the difference between having a hobby and starting a business. Price can't be based on the cost of materials and the time you invest alone. It must be based on the individuality and beauty of your products. Just as any manufacturer, you should go through a period of product development before you decide just what you want to sell.

Prime your inventiveness with ideas. There are a number of craft books on the market as well as articles in women's magazines that give directions to make everything from pasta picture frames to macramé with macaroni.

You'll find all the pasta you need on the supermarket shelves, but for the more esoteric kinds go shopping in

170

the Italian groceries. When you see all the marvelous sizes and shapes you'll understand why people have created folk art with pasta. Pasta is a folk art. You'll find shells, shells, and more shells in all sizes. You'll find stars and squares and buckles and rings. You'll find butterflies, bow ties, curls, and ribbons. And, you'll be enchanted by flower shapes, heart shapes, and little chickens. Even the noodles that go into an alphabet soup can be made into greeting cards, place cards for parties or dinners, or wall plaques.

You may not get rich on your pasta products, but you should have a perfectly marvelous time making some extra money.

Some of our favorites that we'd consider buying: An octagonal mirror with a very wide octagonal frame of vary-sized shells with lace-like borders of spaghetti twists; a hurricane lamp cylinder of wheels to fit over a candle and cast lacy shadows at a dinner table; delicately trimmed greeting cards, ethnic jewelry with an Indian look or the feeling of filigree.

And we're still amazed by what artists call "pastages," marvelous landscape scenes made from pasta beautiful enough to hang in any room in the house.

Where do you sell your pasta products? From your home, at fairs, and, depending on your product, in a variety of retail stores.

Package your pasta greeting cards twelve to a box and try selling them through retail stores and card shops. If you can make paint and pasta into a piece of art, try the boutiques, gift shops, jewelry stores.

AN APPLE A DAY
STARTS YOUR BUSINESS
ON ITS WAY

Homecrafts are in current vogue and quilts, wood carvings, and other homespun arts from Appalachia have great commercial value. But who says you have to live in the mountains to make the objects of Americana? You can start your own homecraft manufacturing operation right in your kitchen wherever it may be.

While the women of Appalachia have been making dolls for generations using the readily available materials of nature—nuts, corn husks, dough, and apples—to perfect dolls that in modern times have become more collector's items than toys, you can if you are skillful also realize their sales potential.

Of all the natural dolls, our favorites are the apple dolls. The nut dolls are "cute." The dough dolls have a homey charm. The corn-husk dolls are dainty and beautiful but they are among the folk arts of the Middle-

European countries and have recently been imported and sold here. The apple dolls seem largely to be a truly American folk art.

There is an art to "working" the sculpted apple heads into marvelous faces that are funny and wise and kind. Then there is an art to dressing the dolls to add to their character. Apple dolls make beautiful decorative pieces when placed in shadow boxes with miniature period pieces to form a country or Victorian setting.

Apple dolls have one-of-a-kind faces and, depending on your skill at modeling these faces and the attention you pay to the details of dress, the price you place on each doll is purely up to you and what you think consumers will pay.

Your major investment will be, in addition to your basic materials, the clothing and, if you wish, the shadow-box setting for the dolls.

Many of the mountain craftspeople wrap their dolls in corn-husk clothes, which can be dyed easily with Rit dyes. The corn husks go on easily, wrapping around the armatures, and the packaged husks are available in craft shops in most cities. You may prefer to dress the dolls in colorful calico prints or denims, but it does take more time to hand-sew clothes and the dolls should be priced accordingly.

Sell your apple dolls from your home, retail, or through direct mail. The mail-order method might be particularly good since apple dolls are still rather rare in most parts of the country. Local fairs, carnivals, and flea markets are also excellent outlets, but don't overlook the handicraft, antique, and gift stores or the small book and card shops that carry unusual items.

If you live in an area where there are hotels, hotel gift shops might also be a good bet. They very often carry unusual gift items made by area craftspeople. You might also try your local museum gift shop.

In fact, you could ask almost any retail store that carries gift or craft items to put one of your best samples on display and take special orders.

There are dozens of craft books and magazine articles that have instructions on how to make these dolls. Each method is slightly different but essentially the same. Check for these books at your local library (and see our Bibliography), or write to the reader service departments of the magazines requesting any articles or instructions that have been published on the making of these dolls. Meanwhile, here is one method:

HOW TO MAKE AN APPLE DOLL

Ignore those big, beautiful, delicious-looking apples at the supermarket and head for any medium-sized, somewhat round and hard variety such as Winesaps, Baldwins, or the smaller Golden Delicious.

The first step is to peel the apple, then to carve the face. The face is carved in broad planes, down and in for the forehead, flat planes for the sides of the face. The nose is cut in a broad wedge shape, slits are made for the eyes and flaps for the ears.

Soak the heads in salt water and then in lemon juice. This prevents the apple from turning brown. Attach a hook to the back of the head and string up over a radiator, hot air duct, or heater to dry. Air should circulate, so, if necessary, keep a small fan operating. The head should be malleable after one day. Work it like clay, pinching the mouth, nose, eyes, and ears into shape. There will be wrinkles but apple dolls are supposed to look elderly. Hang again to dry. In a week or less the head will be one half the original size and ready to be made into a doll.

Most dolls are made with a sturdy coated wire, flexible enough to be twisted into sitting and standing shapes. A knitting needle will be fine to punch two holes, each from top to bottom, in the apple head. Thread a length of wire (about one foot) from bottom up in one hole then down from the top to the bottom of the second one. This forms the body and the legs. At shoulder height, wrap another length of wire and extend on either side to form the arms. You can now wrap the figures in corn-husk clothes, bending the hands, arms, legs, feet, and body as you wish. Add a corn-husk skirt for the women. Absorbent cotton or angel hair or lamb's wool work well for the hair. Just shape it and glue on. Give a rosy gleam to cheeks and lips with poster paint. Use black ink to add on eyes or use seed beads or cloves.

Once you start working you'll find you can use all kinds of materials to make your apple dolls works of art.

BEAUTY FROM NATURE
IS A NATURAL TO SELL

One of the most interesting success stories in the cosmetic business is Estée Lauder's. Mrs. Lauder was blessed with a beautiful complexion, the kind that comes as a birthright not out of bottles. Yet, she smartly packaged her "secret"—a formulation concocted by a pharmacist relative—and sold it to admiring friends and acquaintances.

Now, Estée Lauder is one of the largest privately owned cosmetic companies in the world where Mrs. Lauder, her husband, sons, and other relatives work with thousands of employees to bring beauty to the consumer.

We're not suggesting that everyone can start out in their kitchen and develop into the queen of the cosmetic world, but if you have an interest in beauty products, you might just find that the gold in your kitchen is very glamorous.

Take a look in the stores and you'll see the trend in beauty preparations, like food, is back to the natural. There is a proliferation of fruit shampoos, fruit facial preparations, and natural scents on the market. Beauty magazines sing the praises of cucumber cleansers, avocado creams, oatmeal masks. The good earth and its products are "in."

Just a few, among dozens and dozens, of possible examples: Barley, bran, or oatmeal are good as water softeners, while pine needles and herbs such as rosemary and basil, and dried flowers such as rose petals, are aromatic and soothing. Package these as Bath Brews in small muslin bags tied tightly with colored string, labeled and ready to be dipped into the tub like a tea bag. Make potpourris from spices and herbs or pomander balls for linen closets or clothing closets. Find good, practical formulas for making natural avocado or almond meal or milk-and-honey natural soaps.

You can promote your products locally through women's groups, at school and charity bazaars, through direct-mail announcements, or a series of small advertisements in your local papers.

Contact drugstores, health-food stores, beauty salons, and fashion boutiques. Retail stores will probably want a display or counter card, which will call for an investment on your part for design and printing. You'll also have to package well for retail sale, but there are jobbers through whom you can obtain the proper bottles and jars wholesale.

All of these costs must be figured into the pricing

and you'll finally understand why cosmetics cost so much when the cost of their actual manufacture is rather low. In fact, you'll have to take into consideration the cost of the ingredients, labor, overhead, advertising, promotion, packaging, marketing costs, and the profit a retail dealer would want, before pricing your line. Unless you are a whiz, we suggest you consult with your accountant or someone who has expertise in this area.

Despite all the new commercial products with natural ingredients, you'll still have a jump on the cosmetic giants when it comes to marketing this kind of formulation. It's a long distance between manufacturing commercial cosmetics and marketing them, which means that the products have to withstand changes in temperature and months sitting on the shelf before they are bought by the consumer. That means preservatives, because natural products are very delicate.

The product you offer can be made with fewer chemicals, can be really fresh and "pure" because you can manufacture smaller batches and get them to the consumer more quickly.

Developing your natural cosmetic line is much like developing a group of favorite recipes. You don't really have to start from scratch. Recipes abound and there are several very good paperback books on natural cosmetics that you can obtain through your library (and see our Bibliography). Other sources include women's magazines, celebrity beauty books, and "health" books. A few hours of research in your library should turn up several basic formulations and with experimentation you can create your own unique line.

Since you're entering the beauty world as a professional, you might also consider working with a local
chemist to perfect your formulations.

One of the best things about starting a kitchen cosmetic business is that ordinary kitchen equipment is
perfect for the job. Of course you'll want to have equipment just for your cosmetic-making, but that's primarily
a matter of keeping business and household materials
separate for tax purposes and working convenience. If
you must you could use pots, pans, mixers, and other
utensils interchangeably without harming your cooking
or your cosmetic products.

The name of your product line is important, too.
Clearing it will call for a lawyer. You may think that
"Nature's Beauty" sounds just fine, but about ten other
people may have had the same thought. Once the name
is clear, register your name and trademark. Your attor-
ney will also inform you of which Food and Drug Administration regulations you must adhere to in making and
labeling your products.

Remember that aesthetics count. You'll want to package your products to have enough eye appeal to result
in buy appeal. You'll also have to determine just what
products you can produce to go into your line at a
profit. Three or four items are enough to start with and
they should be simple and related. Among the simplest
things we can suggest are freshener, lotions, shampoos,
and bath preparations that you can make with common
kitchen foods such as milk and honey, cucumbers,
strawberries, and herbs.

As you research you'll find there are dozens of varieties of cosmetics you can consider for your line. To list some of the major ones:

(1) Alcoholic solutions, which include aftershaves and astringents. These are fairly simple solutions of perfume oil in alcohol and water with "conditioners" added.

(2) Water solutions, which include shampoos, skin fresheners, and bubble baths. These are usually 60 percent water and are very easy to make.

(3) Emulsions, which can be (a) water in oil or (b) oil in water. Oil-in-water solutions are by nature non-greasy, cool, and sink into the skin. Water-in-oil emulsions are rich and bring nourishment to the skin.

(4) Emollient oils, which include the body oils, bath oils, and hair conditioners. These are mixtures of oils and very easy to make.

(5) Clear gels, which are combinations of gum and water-based or alcohol-based solutions.

(6) Stick cosmetics, usually lipsticks.

You can also build your business on one product, creating an item that is unique. Consider, for example, bath soaks, which are particularly good as gift items, good as mail-order items, and could probably be sold through drugstores and health stores.

Since you are selling cosmetics, even though they are natural products, you'll still have to check for FDA regulations on labeling. Also check if there are any special taxes in your state which you are liable for if you retail directly yourself.

BIBLIOGRAPHY

FOOD PREPARATION

The Fannie Farmer Cookbook
(Little, Brown and Company, Boston, Mass.)

Betty Crocker's Desserts Cookbook
(Golden Press, New York)

Claiborne, Craig
New York Times Menu Cookbook
(Harper & Row, New York)

Patten, Marguerite
Classic Dishes Made Simple
(Nash Publishing Corp., Los Angeles, California)

Duffy, Patrick Gavin
The Official Mixer's Manual
(Revised & enlarged by James A. Beard)

The Sunset Appetizer Book
(Sunset Book, Lane Books, Menlo Park, California)

Baker's Cut-Up Cake Party Book
(General Foods, Kankakee, Ill.)

SELF-EMPLOYMENT

Gibson, Mary Bass
The Family Circle Book of Careers at Home
(Cowles Book Co., Inc., New York)

Matthews
ON YOUR OWN
(Vintage Books Edition, New York)

Feinman, Jeffrey
100 Surefire Businesses You Can Start with Little or No Money
(Playboy Press, Chicago)

Clark, Leta
Making Money with Your Crafts
(William Morrow, New York)

APPLE SCULPTURES

Horowitz, Eleanor Lander
Mountain People, Mountain Crafts
(J. B. Lippincott, Philadelphia, 1974)

McCall's Needlework & Crafts Christmas Make-It Ideas, V. XVIII
(McCall's Pattern Company, New York, 1974)

GREEN GOLD

Kramer, Jack
The Pit & Pot Grower's Book
(Thomas Y. Crowell Company, New York)

Langer, Richard W.
The After Dinner Gardening Book
(Collier Books, New York)

CANDY IS DANDY

Van Arsdale, M. B., and Emellos, Ruth Parrish
Candy Recipes and Other Confections
(Dover Publications, New York)

CANNING AND PRESERVING

Better Homes and Gardens Home Canning Cook Book
(Meredith Corporation, Des Moines, Iowa)

Borella, Ann
Home Canning and Preserving: The Safe Way
(Cornerstone Library, New York)

Home Canning
(Sunset Book, Lane Books, Menlo Park, California)

Heriteau, Jacqueline
Home Canning and Freezing
(Grosset & Dunlap, New York)

Byron, Mary
Jams & Jellies
(Dover Publications, Inc., New York)

Hertzberg, Ruth; Vaughn, Beatrice; and Greene, Janet
Putting Food By
(The Stephen Greene Press, Brattleboro, Vt.)

Schuler, Elizabeth Meriwether and Stanley
Preserving the Fruits of the Earth
(Galahad Books, New York)

DIRECT MAIL

Martyn, Sean
How to Start and Run a Successful Mail Order Business
(David McKay Company, Inc., New York)

PASTA IS PERFECT

Mergaler, Karen
Noodle Doodle, The Art of Creating with Pasta
(Folk Art Studios, El Toro, California)

A KNACK WITH DOUGH

The Dough It Yourself Handbook
(Morton Salt Company, Chicago, Illinois)

Cross, Linda and John
Kitchen Crafts
(Collier Books, New York)

Too Good To Eat! The Art of Dough Sculpture
(Folk Art Studios, El Toro, California)

Wiseman, Ann
Bread Sculpture, The Edible Art
(101 Productions, San Francisco)

RESTAURANTS

Groff, Betty, and Wilson, Jose
Good Earth and Country Cooking
(Stackpole Books, Harrisburg, Pa.)

Kaufman, William I.
The Tea Cookbook
(Doubleday & Co., Garden City, N.Y.)

Gray, M., and de lo Padua, Vass
How to Be a Success in the Restaurant Business
(Nelson-Hall, Chicago, Ill.)

Opening a Small Restaurant
Small Business Administration, Government Printing Office, Washington)

NATURAL FOODS

Goldbeck, Nikki
Cooking What Comes Naturally
(Cornerstone Library)

Firth, Grace
Living the Natural Life
(Simon and Schuster, New York)

BEAUTY FROM NATURE

Traven, Beatrice
The Complete Book of Natural Cosmetics
(Pocket Books, 1976)

Tucker, Ann
Potpourri, Incense and Other Fragrant Concoctions
(Workman Publishing Company, New York)

Bramson, Ann Sela
Soap—Making It, Using It, Enjoying It
(Workman Publishing Company, New York)

INDEX

Advertising, 23-27
  catering, 52
  children's party service, 100-101
  direct-mail, 25, 82-86
  radio, 25
  yellow pages of the telephone directory, 24-25, 52
Almond
  and chocolate toffee, 151-152
  cookie cups, 50-51
American Home, 42
Appetizers and hors d'oeuvre, 51-55
  clam delight, hearty, 110-111
  delivery of, 54
  developing specialties, 53
  list of favorites, 55
  lobster canapés, 108
  major investment, 55
  1-2-3 dip, 137
  packaging, 54
  presentation ideas, 53-54
  Swedish meat balls, 109-110
  university clientele, 52-53
Apple dolls, 172-175

Apricot
  frosting, 118
  tea bars, 117-118
Avocado plants, 157-158

Baker's Cut-Up Cake Party Book, 121
Banana shake, thick, 95
Banking, 19-20
Bean salad, 134
Beard, James, 92
Beets, pickled, 94-95
Better Homes & Gardens, 37-38
  readers' recipes published by, 66
Blueberry muffins, 98
Bookkeeping, 18-19
Box lunches, 86-88
Brasserie, The, 87
Bread sticks, whole-wheat, 97-98
Broadsides, 25
Bulletin boards, 25-26
Business libraries, 84
Butter nut balls, 44

Cake decorating, 119-122

187